REMEMBERING MINDEN

REMEMBERING

MINDEN

Echoes of Our Past

JOHN AGAN

THE History PRESS

Published by The History Press
Charleston, SC 29403
www.historypress.net

All images courtesy of the author.

First published 2009

Manufactured in the United States

ISBN 978.1.59629.718.0

Library of Congress Cataloging-in-Publication Data

Agan, John.
Remembering Minden : echoes of our past / John Agan.
p. cm.
Summary: Columns from the Minden press-herald.
ISBN 978-1-59629-718-0
1. Minden (La.)--History. 2. Minden (La.)--Biography. 3. Historic buildings--Louisiana--Minden. 4. Minden (La.)--Buildings, structures, etc. I. Minden press-herald. II. Title.
F379.M56A34 2009
976.3'96--dc22
2009021532

CONTENTS

INTRODUCTION

In 2000, I was given the wonderful opportunity to write a weekly column on local history in the *Minden Press-Herald*. In the subsequent nine years, it has been my pleasure to recount stories of old Minden and Webster Parish with my readers, while at the same time learning so much about local history from those readers as they shared their memories and tales handed down through the generations. Now, I have been given the chance to share some of those stories in this volume. I hope my readers will enjoy these selected stories of Minden's heritage.

Juanita Murphy Agan, June 28, 1923–October 12, 2008.

The title of my newspaper column is "Echoes of Our Past"; I have carried that title over to this book. The name was not chosen lightly. As a teacher of history, I truly believe that the lessons of history are invaluable in helping our society succeed. As such, my topics are always chosen because the events that took place in the past recounted in my articles can have some application to our present lives. Keep that in mind as you read these stories.

I owe thanks to so many people for sharing their knowledge with me on local history that it would be impossible to thank them all; however, I need to dedicate this book to the memory of my mother, Juanita Murphy Agan, who died in October 2008. She was the driving force and inspiration behind my love of history. She would be so proud to have seen this book published and I publish in honor of her memory.

CHAPTER 1

THE FOUNDING OF MINDEN

One important milepost in the history of every community is the date of its founding. Most communities choose to date their founding from their formal date of incorporation, which, while not the actual beginning of the settlement of the town, is an easy date to reference through formal records. In the case of Homer, a town created to be a parish seat, the incorporation date and the time of first settlement were actually very closely spaced in time. Here in Minden we have normally considered our founding to have occurred with the first settlers on our current town site. Minden was incorporated in 1854, yet the roots of the community had begun nearly twenty years before that date. This "Echo of Our Past" will attempt to examine the founding of Minden. Normally an article like this would be expected to claim to shed a little light on the origins of the town. Yet in our case, the founding of Minden is a historical event that seems harder to tie down the more it is examined.

When researching the history of our immediate area of Louisiana, two sources are considered "definitive." These works, published about 1890, are Harris and Hulse's *History of Claiborne Parish* and *Biographical and Historic Memoirs of Northwest Louisiana*. So let's examine these two authorities to determine the date of our founding. Harris and Hulse's book, considered the better of the two sources, gives the following information about the founding of Minden: "This beautiful and thriving little city was founded in the year 1837, by Charles H. Veeder." So there we have the answer, and a very short article for today. But we need to check the other authority to verify this information. *Biographical and Historic Memoirs* was written largely as a vanity publication, with subscribers paying to have their biographies published in a volume. However, the introductory material on each parish gives some of the most detailed glimpses of the history of our region. In the Webster Parish section of this work it asserts: "The town site formed, practically, part and parcel of the wilderness up to 1837, when Charles H. Veeder, a native of Schenectady, N.Y., born there on October 1, 1796, and a soldier of 1812, established his store here and determined to make the place the center of trade and justice for Claiborne." So both sources have been compared and they agree that 1837 is the date of Minden's establishment. Unfortunately, we continue reading on the page and find some interesting tidbits.

Biographical and Historic Memoirs goes on to state that Veeder's son-in-law, Myles Fisher, was named postmaster of Minden in 1837. Historically, post offices were not created immediately after the founding of a community. The awarding of a post office in 1837 would seem to indicate that the settlement had existed prior to that date. Later in its pages, the same book discusses the peaceful settlement of a long-running land dispute between Veeder and Reuben Drake. The author gives early 1837 as the date of this settlement. So if this dispute had been ongoing and was settled in 1837, it would seem to indicate that Veeder must have settled prior to that date.

The best answer seems to be to move forward to other sources to verify the date of 1837. One source might be to check for any record left by the undisputed founder of Minden, Charles Veeder. Veeder left Minden in 1849 for California, where he later founded two additional towns before his death in 1875 in Bakersfield, California. Over the past few years, I have been in contact with the descendants of Charles Veeder in California. They never knew that their ancestor had lived in Louisiana or that he had founded a community here. In fact, they have no tangible evidence of Mr. Veeder, not even a picture or any written document. So the "horse's mouth" for the founding of Minden is silent on the subject. The next step is to turn to secondary sources of information.

The first person to assemble an organized history of Minden was Dr. Luther Longino. In his 1930 work, *Thoughts, Visions and Sketches of North Louisiana*, he tells us: "The site upon which Minden now stands was purchased from A.L. Stewart by Charles L. Veeder in 1835, and a building was erected." That date seems more in line with the establishment of a post office and with the land dispute resulting from the purchase of the same land by both Veeder and Drake. It also corresponds with another statement by Longino that J.W. Berry arrived in the area in 1835 and arrived in time to see the laying out of the settlement of Minden. Longino used as his sources Burton Miller, Elisha

Nickerson and Mark Talton, all pioneer settlers of the area. Thus, Longino was the only one to both cite his sources and apparently to talk extensively of the founding of the town with the old-timers. This alone gives his date some additional credence. Later, Longino moves the date forward when he adds: "The town was laid off by Veeder in 1836, comprising all that level table land, beginning at Prothro Branch and extending east half a mile or more, and outlined on both sides by branches running parallel half a mile apart, thus separating the old town site from the several subdivisions incorporated since that day."

A third vital source of local history is the "Centennial Edition" of the *Minden Signal-Tribune*. This paper was published on December 31, 1934, in honor of the centennial of something. What was being celebrated? It would seem that the paper was claiming 1834 or the start of 1835 as the date of Minden's founding, but such is not clearly stated. The paper carefully states that it is celebrating the beginning of settlement in Webster Parish, but doesn't give what event it is using to date that settlement. By 1835, Newt Drew had been living on the site of Overton for well over a decade and Overton was well established as a community. In fact, it became the seat of government for Claiborne Parish in 1836. It would seem that the paper was implying that the celebrated event was the founding of Minden. We will next examine the historical evidence contained in this newspaper to see if it clears up the mystery.

Isaac Murrell, the first European child born in northwest Louisiana, wrote a short history of Claiborne Parish for the *Webster Tribune* before his death in the 1870s. While he was a boy in what is still Claiborne Parish at the time of Minden's founding, Murrell was close enough to be a very good source for information about the subject. He agrees with two other sources and places the date of founding as 1837. Yet Murrell has quite a few pieces of contradictory information in his writing, and also seems confused about the facts surrounding Charles Veeder, so we need to see what other sources in this paper state. On the same page as Murrell's article, a quarter-page ad for Judge J. Frank McInnis gives the date of Minden's founding as 1832. While this is certainly not a reliable source, it indicates some of the confusion prevailing about the founding time of our town among even the most prominent Mindenites of the era.

Also contained in the paper is an article written by Judge Lynn K. Watkins in 1908, outlining the history of Minden. Watkins's father, John D. Watkins, came to Minden in 1850 to teach at the Minden Male Academy, and later became a distinguished attorney and judge. His family credentials alone make his account worth examining. Watkins dates the founding of Minden as occurring in 1836. He uses as his source the first known plat map of Minden, made by Claiborne Parish surveyor Williamson Jones. The only current copies of this map are dated September 5, 1851. On that date, Jones affirmed that version as a copy of his original map, but he doesn't give the date of his original survey. Watkins reveals that his copy of the map gives the 1836 date and uses the name Minden, moving the date of founding several months ahead of the previously cited 1837.

Another unsigned article in the paper also uses the date 1837, and a letter written to the *Minden Democrat* in 1873 by Pike Reynolds, who had operated a business in Minden in the 1840s, dates Minden as being founded prior to 1838. There seems to be little doubt of that fact, based on the establishment of a post office and the appropriation made for the Minden Academy by the Louisiana legislature in 1838.

Several accounts in the paper deal with the founding of Germantown. It seems very clear that the establishment of Germantown and the birth of Minden have some connection. I have an unproven personal theory that Charles Veeder came in contact with the Germantown colonists on their way to Louisiana from Pennsylvania. Veeder was living in southern Indiana, near the Ohio River. He did much of his business in the Kentucky port of Louisville on the Ohio. The Germantown settlers came down the Ohio to Louisiana. When the colony reached its eventual home in Louisiana, all sources agree that Veeder was close behind. Some have even claimed that Veeder led the colonists to the site, although the best evidence rejects that theory. All sources place the arrival of the Germantown colonists in our area in 1835 at the latest. It would seem that Veeder must have arrived here sooner than 1837.

These facts dating from the 1870s forward make a confusing picture. Yet other factors have added to the problem of pinning down the date of Minden's establishment. During the 1970s, a letter was received here in Minden by the Webster Parish Library. A gentleman in New Jersey was hoping to sell an old invoice he had found in family papers in the attic. The invoice was for some supplies purchased from an unnamed business. However, the name of the community was clearly visible on the paper as Minden, Louisiana. The date on the invoice was 1834, months before it was thought that Minden had been in existence.

In short, the exact founding of Minden may always remain a mystery. Was it in 1834, as claimed by the never seen but described invoice in New Jersey, or 1837, as several respected sources assert, or perhaps 1835, as indicated by the local sesquicentennial celebration in 1985? We do know that by 1837, a post office was here, so the town was in existence. However, we cannot yet determine when Charles Veeder came to the area and, in the words of Burton Miller, "forever ruined one of the finest and best deer stands in all the country." That pivotal event in our history may forever remain an elusive "Echo of Our Past."

CHAPTER 2
THE MINDEN MALE ACADEMY

Recently, through the efforts of the Minden Residential Historic District under the leadership of their president, Schelley Brown, a state historic marker was erected in Academy Park. The marker tells the story of the park, which was the home of the topic of this "Echo," the Minden Male Academy.

An often-confused fact in Minden history is the difference between the two major antebellum educational institutions in our town, the Minden Male Academy and the Minden Female College. Most of the attention locally has been paid to the Female College, an institution that earned a South-wide reputation for academic excellence and attracted students from as far away as Ohio. However, the legacy of the Minden Male Academy is equally distinguished, and although it didn't offer college-level courses, it actually operated for a longer period than the Female College and numbered many distinguished men among its faculty and alumni.

The foundations of both the Minden Male Academy and the Minden Female College began in 1838 with the establishment of the Minden Academy. This institution received an appropriation of $1,500 from the Louisiana legislature to erect a building at Minden for "academic purposes." The idea of a school was originated by Charles H. Veeder, the founder of Minden, who worked with area ministers to set up this school. Minden was one of the few communities in Louisiana to have a school that could be considered, at least in part, public. The Reverend R.T. Boggs was the first teacher and the school was located on what is today the site of Minden High School. The decision to remodel and expand the Minden High School facility on the existing site assured that those grounds would serve as home to a school into the seeable future, just as they have for the past 169 years. The second principal of the school was Henry M. Spofford, who became a prominent attorney after leaving Minden. During the years of Reconstruction, Spofford became a key member of the "Redeemer" movement in Louisiana Democratic Party politics. Henry Spofford later served on the Louisiana State Supreme Court. Spofford was followed at the Minden Academy by Mr. Burke, the Reverend William Brooks and finally the Reverend W.H. Scales. While the school was by nature a private school, the state appropriation required that part of the original $1,500 be used to create a fund to pay for the education of indigent students. The Minden Academy operated for about 12 years, until 1850. In that year, political considerations made changes in the structure of the school necessary.

The Louisiana Constitution of 1845 made the use of any public funds for the benefit of private schools, including the indigent student fund, illegal. The Minden Academy continued to operate for about five years without the state funds until it was reorganized in 1850. At that time, local civic leaders, led by W. Abner Drake, decided to split the institution into two separate schools, one for males and another for females. The Minden Male Academy was built with funds given by Drake on a plot of land he donated for the school. Later, in July 1852, Drake, Drury Murrell, J. Gibbs and T. Gibbs donated an additional 80 2/3 acres to the Male Academy to complete the campus. Today, the campus of that school is Academy Park. The apparent idea behind the split was that the female school could be expanded to include college-level courses and attract enrollment from outside the area. It was in this same period that the Mansfield Female College, which endured into the twentieth century before merging into Centenary College, was established.

At first, the Male Academy and the Female Seminary (as it was originally known) operated under the same headmaster. Some accounts list the first president of the two schools as John S. Garvin; however, most sources name John D. Watkins as the first head of both institutions. Born in Caldwell County, Kentucky, in 1828, Watkins graduated from Cumberland College and came to Louisiana as a teacher. While holding his position at the Minden Male Academy, he read law at night and was admitted to the bar in 1852. That same year, he was named district attorney and gave up his post at the college. He later had a distinguished career as an attorney and public official, serving as district judge, state senator and delegate to the Louisiana Constitutional Convention in 1879, in addition to being the Democratic nominee for Congress from the Fourth District in 1874.

The main building of the Minden Male Academy in an image taken after the Civil War.

Upon Watkins's resignation from the Minden Male Academy, his assistant, A.B. George, became principal. Like Watkins, George had been reading law at night and was admitted to the bar in 1855, and then gave up his post at the academy. Born in Wilcox County, Alabama, in 1828, he first met J.D. Watkins at Cumberland College, where they were both students. George graduated in 1850 and came to Minden to work with Watkins. After leaving the academy, he served as an alderman and mayor of Minden, while engaged in a law practice with Watkins. George also served as editor of the *Minden Democrat* and as district attorney, state senator, district judge and along with Watkins was a delegate to the Constitutional Convention of 1879. Eventually, George left Minden for Shreveport after being elected to the State Court of Appeals.

Separate leadership of the Male Academy and the Female College seems to have begun in 1853, when the Female Seminary was reorganized as the Minden Female College. Professor Slack was named president of the Female College, while George remained the head of the Male Academy.

In later years, the Male Academy had other outstanding leaders. W.E. Paxton headed the school in the years immediately after the Civil War. Paxton was also the pastor of the Minden Baptist Church while leading the academy. He was a leader among Louisiana Baptists and wrote what is still considered the definitive history of the early years of the Baptist Church in Louisiana.

Sumpter D. Spann served as an instructor at the Minden Male Academy for many years before becoming the principal of the institution in the 1880s. Spann was remembered for coming to class each day with a bundle of switches. Usually he managed to use all of these switches as tools of discipline before the day ended. About 1870, Professor Spann built the home that is today the residence of Mrs. J.W. Dickinson on Pennsylvania Avenue. The street leading to this home bears Spann's name.

Among the graduates of the Minden Male Academy were some of the leading citizens of north Louisiana. John T. Watkins, son of J.D. Watkins, and John N. Sandlin, both graduates of the academy, had remarkably similar political careers. Both served as district attorney and district judge, and were elected to eight terms each in the United States House of Representatives. Sandlin's brother, McIntyre Sandlin, another alumnus, served as mayor of Minden and as Webster Parish tax assessor for twenty-eight years. Thomas W. Fuller Jr., longtime Minden newspaper editor and superintendent of Webster Parish schools, graduated from the Minden Male Academy in the 1870s. William G. Stewart, president of the Webster Parish School Board, for

Students of the Minden Male Academy in the 1880s.

Students of the Minden Male Academy in 1895, shortly before the institution closed.

The main building of the Minden Male Academy after it had been moved and spent seventy years as a home and boardinghouse.

whom Stewart Elementary School was named, was also an alumnus of the Male Academy, as was David W. Pratt, a two-term sheriff of Webster Parish. Members of such leading local families as the Drakes, Drews, Crichtons and Webbs also were alumni of the school. In fact, nearly all the business and governmental leaders in Minden in the years between the end of the Civil War and the first decades of the twentieth century were homegrown products of the Minden Male Academy.

The Minden Academy operated successfully for many years, well into the 1890s, after the Female College had been closed and reopened in another form as a business school. Ironically, a change in the Louisiana Constitution in 1845 had brought about the creation of the Minden Male Academy and another change in the Constitution, taking place in 1898, caused its demise. Provisions of that state charter required that public school systems be created. In Minden, the Male Academy and the women's school were combined to form the new Minden Public School, which met in the old Female College buildings. This school became Minden High School shortly after 1900.

After the death of the Male Academy, the property was converted into a park. The original building constructed by Drake was purchased for fifty dollars at auction in May 1903 by John T. Watkins. He had the building remodeled and moved to the corner of East and West and Sullivan. It served for many years as the home of a granddaughter of John D. Watkins. Eventually, it became an apartment house that earned the nickname the "Honeymoon Hotel" because so many young married couples from Minden made their first homes in the building. When that building was torn down in the 1970s, the last tangible artifact of the Minden Male Academy vanished from Minden. However, the name of that school has lived on in Academy Park, named for the institution of learning on that site for a half century. The Minden Male Academy, while not as well known as the Minden Female College, is also a very significant "Echo of Our Past" that has finally received a tangible indication of its history with the new marker.

CHAPTER 3

THE MINDEN BAPTIST CHURCH

This "Echo of Our Past" will detail the history of the largest church in Minden, the First Baptist Church. The Minden Baptist Church (the name First Baptist Church of Minden was not adopted until March 1924) was organized on December 29, 1844. Two sessions were held that day under the leadership of two men from the Rehoboth Church of Mt. Lebanon, Elders W.J. Larkin and L.L. Washburne. At first the church was organized with four charter members, R.L. Horn, Phebe Bird, Thomas Lovel and Sarah Drew. It seems likely that this meeting was held in the home of Mrs. Drew. From these beginnings, the church grew, as in the second session on that day two new members were accepted: Lucy Ann Morrow by experience and Emily Sligh by letter from another Baptist church. Over the next year, the small congregation in what was then a community on the frontier, less than fifty miles from the international border with the Republic of Texas, continued to increase in size. In August 1845, the first black member, Nancy, a "servant of Sister Allen," joined the Minden Baptist Church; other slaves would follow over the next few years. The next month the membership was decreased by one, when a certain member (names will be withheld to protect the innocent, even though it happened 158 years ago) of the congregation was excluded from fellowship for "drunkenness and gambling." The first pastor of the church was George Washington Bains, grandfather of President Lyndon Baines Johnson (Bains added the "e" to his name after moving to Texas).

In 1846, the church moved into its first house of worship, located on what is today the southeast corner of the intersection of Lee Street and Broadway. That building was the home of the congregation for the next

George Washington Bains, first pastor of the Minden Baptist Church and great-grandfather of President Lyndon Baines Johnson.

fifty-six years, longer than any other house of worship. As Minden grew, the Minden Baptist Church grew along with it, slowly but steadily. A major disruption of the church membership came in 1865 and 1866, when nearly 50 members of the congregation, freed slaves, were granted letters of dismissal to unite with the newly formed St. Rest's Baptist Church. By 1878, the church rolls listed 54 members, but over the next decade the membership more than doubled, as by the end of 1889, there were 113 persons affiliated with the Minden Baptist Church. During these years, problems began to surface with the church building. One recurrent problem was keeping up the fence around the church property. as hogs were in the habit of entering the church property and staying under the church building. Apparently this was a problem throughout Minden, as in 1902 the city placed a bounty on stray hogs and also required owners to register the animals with the town government. Besides these livestock concerns, the church building was also becoming too small for the congregation and upkeep was also a problem.

In 1901, the new Minden Mill of the Bodcau Lumber Company opened in town and brought a newfound prosperity. The Minden Baptist Church became financially able to construct a new building, an impressive brick

The original church building of the Minden Baptist Church, shown after it had been converted to a residence.

structure located on what is today the front parking lot of the Minden Medical Center on Main Street. When the church entered this building in 1902, the membership had grown to 200 persons. That church building became better known to most local residents in its second capacity, because after the church built a third home in 1925, the second house of worship was later remodeled and became the Rex Theatre. The 1902 building was remarkable for its indoor baptistery, with glass walls and the first electric lights in our church. After entering the new building, membership stabilized and actually dropped. By the time the annual report to the Liberty Baptist Association was compiled in 1911, membership had fallen to 183 members. In that year alone, the church had a net loss of 21 members, or more than 10 percent of the congregation.

By 1917, as the United States entered World War I, membership had grown to 389 persons. Of that number, 239 were female and 150 were male. In the years immediately after World War I, Minden and the church began a period of rapid growth. By 1924, it was clear that the Minden Baptist Church had outgrown its relatively new home. The first church building had been used for fifty-six years, while the second was only home to the

BAPTIST CHURCH, MINDEN, LA.

The 1902 building of the Minden Baptist Church.

congregation for twenty-three years. In preparation for building a new church home, the congregation reorganized in the early spring of 1924, and its newly chartered name became the First Baptist Church of Minden. The English property at the corner of Broadway and First Street was purchased as a site for the new church building. (An aside here, in case anyone ever wondered why Minden has a series of streets numbered First, Second and Third beginning in the middle of town—it's because of an error in reading a map. According to letters from the children of Isaac Murrell, who lived on Pennsylvania Avenue at the end of First Street, the original name was I Street, indicating that it was the ninth street in a progression of downtown streets following the alphabet. At some point, after the other letter streets had acquired new names, some mapmaker read that name as First Street and the name stuck. By the way, the Murrell children chose the name Pennsylvania Avenue for the street in front of their home because they knew the White House was located on Pennsylvania Avenue in Washington and they wanted their home to be on an equally prestigiously named street.)

Aided greatly by the philanthropy of Joseph G. and Nancy Mullins Ferguson, the new home of the First Baptist Church was completed and ready to be occupied by the end of April 1925. The first event in the church had actually happened in February, when church organist Miss Lavinia Shealy was married to Mr. Bert David in the unfurnished church. Miss Lavinia had been determined to have her wedding in the new church, and she was not going to let the absence of pews and finishing work interrupt her plans. The first event in the church after completion was the funeral of former U.S. congressman John T. Watkins of Minden, a former president of the Louisiana Baptist Convention. When the church moved into the new building in 1925, its membership had swelled to 832 members, an increase of more than 100 percent in eight years. This rapid growth continued unchecked over the next few years. In 1927, the Ferguson family funded the construction of a huge metal tabernacle, a unique feature of the Minden community for fifty years. By 1939, the church boasted 1,816 members and was one of the largest Southern Baptist churches in Louisiana. The all-time peak membership was recorded four years later, in 1943, when the church roll included the names of 2,246 persons.

The 1925 building of the First Baptist Church of Minden.

The Ferguson Memorial Tabernacle of the First Baptist Church of Minden, 1927–76.

In 1944, the First Baptist Church of Minden celebrated its centennial and also played host to the annual meeting of the Louisiana Baptist Convention. That marked the fifth, and most likely the final, time that the local church served as host. In the years since, the demand for convention facilities and hotel rooms has made the convention too large an event for all but the largest communities in our state. That year also marked a change in the way membership numbers were reported by Louisiana Baptist churches. From that point forward, churches reported two categories: resident members and non-resident members who had moved from the community but had not moved their church membership. In 1944, the First Baptist Church reported a total membership of 2,396, but a resident membership of 1,448. In the years after the war, resident membership continued to boom. By 1949, it had reached a peak of 1,614 members. Over the next few years, the membership dropped off a little as the religious community in Minden grew. The Sibley Road Mission of the First Baptist Church was established, taking members from the mother congregation. That church later became the Southside Baptist Church and is today the North Acres Baptist Church. One other local church, the Germantown Baptist Church, began as a mission of First Baptist. In addition, other Southern Baptist churches were established in Minden, so although Minden was growing, the membership at FBC did not keep pace.

During the 1960s, growth began again at First Baptist. Dr. Ronald Prince was called as pastor in November 1966, and his dynamic leadership sparked a new time of increase. Resident membership climbed back over the 1,600 mark for the first time in nearly a decade in 1969, and by the time Dr. Prince retired from the pulpit in 1987, it had reached 1,882. In 1977, under his leadership, the church moved into its fourth church building, which is still in use by the congregation. Today, under the leadership of our pastor, the Reverend Wayne Dubose, we are enjoying a new period of growth with a resident membership of over 1,920.

Well by now you might be wondering what the point of all these numbers might be. Am I just stuck on statistics and trying to brag about the size of my church? While I do confess a fondness for statistics, there is another, higher purpose. These numbers I have listed are not merely marks on a paper; they stand for people, thousands of people. The First Baptist Church of Minden has carried on its rolls more than two thousand names for more than sixty years. Those thousands of members have touched the life of our community in so many ways and have helped create the "Echoes of Our Past."

CHAPTER 4
THE MINDEN FEMALE COLLEGE

The foundations of the Minden Female College began in 1838 with the establishment of the Minden Academy. This institution was partially funded by an appropriation of $1,500 passed by the Louisiana legislature to erect a building in Minden for "academic purposes." The idea of a school was originated by Charles H. Veeder, the founder of Minden, who used his influence with members of the legislature to gain approval of the stipend. Veeder's plan was to found a town and have the seat of government for the county or parish established in his settlement, and thus attract new citizens for the community. His initial efforts to have Minden named the seat of Claiborne Parish failed when that distinction went to Overton. Failing to win the county seat caused Veeder to change his focus toward the building of churches and schools to attract settlers. Later, after Overton was abandoned as parish seat because of its unhealthy environment, Veeder again tried unsuccessfully to have Minden named parish seat. On that occasion, the honor went to Homer, another town specifically created in order to become the seat of government. After Minden's second failure to become parish seat, Veeder encountered financial difficulties and relocated to California during the gold rush of 1849. While living there, his plan to develop a county seat failed on two other occasions. He was living in California in 1871, when Minden finally became the seat of the new parish of Webster.

Veeder probably never realized that the legacy he left behind in Minden, while not achieving his specific goal, helped create a thriving community that occupied a leading position in business, religion and education in north Louisiana. The most influential institution that Veeder helped create in Minden was the Minden Academy. Veeder worked with area ministers to set up this school. The Reverend R.T. Boggs was the first teacher and the school was located on what is today the College Street site of Minden High School. While the school was by nature a private school, the state appropriation required that part of the original $1,500 be used to create a fund to pay for the education of indigent students. The Minden Academy operated for about twelve years, until 1850. In that year, political considerations made changes in the structure of the school necessary.

The Louisiana Constitution of 1845 made the use of any public funds for the benefit of private schools, including the indigent student fund, illegal. The school continued to operate for about five years without the state funds, until it was reorganized after the town of Minden was incorporated in 1850. At that time, local civic leaders, led by W. Abner Drake, decided to split the institution into two separate schools, one for males and another for females. The Minden Male Academy was constructed from funds donated by Drake and on a plot of land he donated for the school. Today, the campus of that school is Academy Park. The Minden Male Academy operated for many years, and provided the primary and secondary school education for many of the leading citizens of Minden during the late nineteenth and early twentieth centuries.

The other school founded in Minden during 1850 also was largely funded by the Drake family. In fact, the school was originally called the Mahala Seminary, named after Abner Drake's wife. Soon, however, the institution came to be known as the Minden Female Seminary. At first the Male Academy and the Female Seminary apparently operated under the same headmaster. Local tradition names John D. Watkins as the first head of both institutions. Supporting this tradition is the later locations of the homes of the children of John D. Watkins. Both sons, Congressman John T. Watkins and Justice Lynn K. Watkins of the State Court of Appeals, lived between the two campuses on College Street. Soon after John D. Watkins's time as headmaster, the school was headed by A.B. George, who later served on the State Supreme Court of Louisiana. Separate leadership seems to have begun in 1852, when John S. Garvin was appointed president of the seminary. Garvin served for about eighteen months until Professor S.L. Slack was elected president in August 1853.

Under the leadership of Professor Slack, a move was begun to change the status of the seminary to that of a full-fledged college. This idea became a reality on March 16, 1854, when the Louisiana legislature passed Act 245, creating the Minden Female College. Part of the charter of the act of incorporation read:

> *Section 1—Be it enacted by the Senate and House of Representatives of the State of Louisiana in general assembly convened, that John M. Sandidge, John L. Hodges and Dr. John R. Evans, of the Parish of Bossier and James M. Morrow, Dr. J.W. Quarles, Isaac Murrell, Charles Chaffe, Dr. James D. Harper, Henry Carleton, Dr. Daniel McFarland, Isaac F. Sibley, William M. Smith, J.L. Slack, and Dr. Alexander McIntyre of the Parish of Claiborne, and their successors in office be, and they are hereby created and constituted a body politic and corporate, by name and style of the Trustees of the Minden Female College, a Seminary of Learning for Females, situated in the Town of Minden, in Claiborne Parish in the State of Louisiana.*

The new college acquired all assets of the Female Seminary, including the campus and buildings, and the seminary ceased to exist. On February 26, 1855, the legislature passed Act 14, which appropriated $5,000 for the college. This act required that as many as eight indigent students be admitted to the four-year course of study at no charge. The balance of this appropriation, along with local allocations, gifts and contributions, permitted the school to keep its charges for tuition and room and board relatively low.

The Minden Female College was located on what is today the site of the 1953 Minden High School Building and the previous location of the 1910 Minden Public School Building. The main building of the school was a large, two-story Greek Revival structure, flanked by two smaller buildings on each side. Large trees dominated the front lawn of the school and a white picket fence ran across the front of the property along the road. The building was two bays wide, with four two-story Doric columns and pediments and a gabled roof. It had two narrow wings connected to the main building by halls, containing tall ceiling-to-floor windows, with separate doorways in the center of each wing. On both the east and west sides of the main structure were additional two-story buildings, with a façade similar to the main building but having hipped roofs.

The school's classrooms were located on the first floor of the central hall and the left wing. Students and teachers lived on the second floor of the central hall. The right wing contained a parlor and an apartment for faculty members. The Concert Hall, located to the east of the central structure, was the scene of many community meetings, in addition to the program and concerts. During the Civil War, students of the college and officers from the Confederate forces stationed at Camp Magruder east of town staged dramatic productions in the Concert Hall. In October 1902, about six years before it was torn down, the Concert Hall hosted the Louisiana

The 1875 graduating class of the Minden Female College at its twentieth reunion in 1895.

Baptist Convention, when the new home of the First Baptist Church was not completed in time for the meeting. The numerous functions that were held in the Concert Hall contributed to Minden's reputation as a cultured city. The structure located just west of the main building served as the president's home for most of the school's existence. Some records indicate that at various times this building may also have been used for dormitory space or classrooms.

Female students of all ages attended the Female College, and a diploma was considered a college degree, although the curriculum would not be considered at the collegiate level today. Along with fundamental education classes, the school taught courses in chemistry, Latin, astronomy, higher mathematics, history, art, drama and music. Traditional accounts say that Professor Slack hired several teachers from the famous Julliard School of Music in 1854. Among these instructors was a Professor J. Luther, a German, who gave concerts in which he performed on the piano and the organ simultaneously. During those years there were sixty girls studying piano, organ and violin at the school.

The school employed strict discipline and the students kept a rigid schedule, including devotions, classes, needlework and study. Girls boarding at the school were allowed to have visitors on Sundays and "dates" were chaperoned. Mrs. Thomas Campbell collected several interesting stories about student life in those days. One tells of a young man who came from Mississippi to find lodging for his sister, who planned to attend the Minden College. He met and fell in love at first sight with the daughter of the house where his sister was to board. He later married the young lady. Another tale is of a girl who eloped in the traditional way by climbing out of her window using a rope made of bedsheets. This action caused her to be disowned by her family.

Under the direction of Slack, the first class graduated on July 20, 1855. The members of this class were E.A.R. Brown of Natchitoches Parish, Emily L. Garrison of Minden, Penelope L. Hodges of Bossier Parish, Anna L. Harper of Claiborne Parish, Augusta L. Long of Claiborne Parish, Mary A. McIntyre of Minden and Martha E. Sullivan of Homestead, Arkansas. The *Webster Tribune* of September 27, 1883, remembered that occasion as follows: "The commencement was a grand affair in Minden. Slavery was then at its zenith, and hundreds of splendid equipages were seen on the streets and evidences of wealth were seen everywhere."

Professor Slack left the school in 1856, and was succeeded by Professor J. Franklin Ford on October 5, 1856. Ford was a graduate of Cumberland University and also served as the minister at the Minden Presbyterian Church. For the next few years, the college obtained most of its faculty through ties to the Presbyterian Church. Many of these instructors had Ivy League educational backgrounds, and the quality of its instructors helped the college enjoy its Golden Age in those antebellum years under Ford. Professor Ford claimed that the school made a profit of $60,000 during his tenure from 1856 to 1862. In 1860, internal problems arose at the school. That year, sixteen girls were scheduled to graduate, but only six participated in the ceremony. The other ten boycotted the event in protest over how Ford had determined the first honor student. The controversy grew and began to affect the enrollment of the school. Several trustees demanded Ford's resignation, but when the board met he was retained by a single vote. In response to this lack of confidence, Ford resigned in February 1862, effective with the end of the academic year. That year eight students completed studies, but only seven took part in graduation exercises, as one young lady refused to accept her diploma if it was to be awarded by Ford. The strife at the conclusion of Ford's tenure, combined with the hardships endured during the Civil War, weakened the school and it never regained the status it had achieved under Franklin Ford in his early years.

Dr. J.E. Bright succeeded Ford as president of the Minden Female College. In addition to his impact on the college itself, Bright and his family made other lasting impacts on the Minden area. His granddaughter married Thomas W. Fuller, a prominent journalist and educator, who served as superintendent of Webster Parish Schools from 1908 until his death in 1920. Bright also established a large farm on the western edge of Minden, along present-day Highway 80 West or the Shreveport Road. This property was later purchased as a homeplace by John Sidney Killen, a prominent leader in religious and government affairs, who was representing Minden in the Louisiana legislature when Webster Parish was created. Bright steered the school through the troubled years of the Civil War. The college remained open during the war, graduating one of its largest classes in 1865, but the music curriculum was eliminated. In 1871, Professor Bright resigned, beginning another time of trouble for the school.

The Reverend T.B. Russell served as president from 1871 to 1872. In 1872, the school was unable to find a suitable president and the board named an interim principal. This principal had two distinctions: she was Mildred Boyle, the first woman to head the school—and perhaps one of the few women to be in charge of an institution of higher learning in the country at that time. In addition to her gender, Miss Boyle also achieved another first: she was an 1858 graduate of the Minden Female College as first honor student, the only alumnus to head the college. Miss Boyle served as principal for the 1872–73 school year and was replaced by Reverend J.C. Deramus, the new president, at the beginning of the 1873–74 term. However, Deramus resigned in December 1873, and Miss Boyle was returned to her previous role of principal. She kept this job for several years. During these years, the Board of Trustees apparently took a more active role in managing the school. Perhaps the tumultuous nature of the Reconstruction years contributed to the difficulty in obtaining permanent male leadership.

Miss Boyle served until 1876, when a new leader was chosen and given the title president. (Mildred Boyle married Samuel Y. Webb in 1884.) Colonel Thomas O. Benton served as head of the Minden Female College from 1876 until 1881. He was succeeded by Colonel George D. Alexander, who also served for five years, leaving in 1886. The next president of the college was Major A.L. Cox. Cox remained at the school until about 1890, when he began publication of a newspaper in Minden, called *Cox's Educational Monthly*. In later years, he purchased the Long Spring's Resort hotel north

Students of the Minden Female College in the 1880s.

of Minden. Professor P.B.H. Shearer was named principal of the school in 1890 after teaching at the Minden Male Academy for a year. He remained at the school until 1896. Shearer's faculty in 1890 included the following individuals: Professor Garrison, Professor Sumpter D. Spann, Mrs. DuBose, Miss Weissler, Mrs. Wrenn and Mrs. Shearer. Records indicate that the average attendance at that time was around one hundred students.

At some point during Shearer's tenure, the school's name was changed to the Minden Normal and Business College, and in 1892, it began sharing its facilities with a new Minden "public school." The new school was taught by Professor Burke and charged tuition of two dollars. By 1900, the college had apparently ceased to exist, as the building was used for what was called a high school, although it did not meet the state standards for such a school. By 1906, when Dr. C.A. Ives was hired as principal of Minden High School, the college facilities were in disrepair.

Ives, who later served for many years as dean of the College of Education at Louisiana State University, converted the local public school into a certified high school and supervised the construction of the three-story brick school building built in 1909–10. In a letter written to R.O. Machen, then assistant superintendent of Webster Parish Schools, in 1953, Ives recalled his first days in Minden. He wrote this letter after reading a newspaper story relating that the cornerstone of that 1909 building had been recently removed. When the stone was opened, the contents had been nearly unrecognizable, because they were stored in a defective metal container. Ives wrote that the cornerstone had contained many important documents, including all the documents placed in the cornerstone of the main building of the Female College in 1854. He also remembered that when he came to Minden in 1906, the 1854 building was still in use. He recalled, "The noble façade was all that was left in good order of the Female College building…walls were soiled and had many chinks." At a public reception, School Board president F.H. Drake asked the then young Ives if he thought the building needed anything. Ives impetuously replied, "Yes, it ought to burn up," a response that he soon realized was "like ice-water on the tender and sentimental feelings of many women who had gotten their education there." It took Ives several months to restore his relations with some of these alumni of the Minden Female College.

During 1909, while the new school building was being built, several of the old buildings were destroyed, while others found new sites and uses. The main building of the college was moved across the street from its former site to the southwest corner of West Union and College Streets. It served as the school for Minden until the new brick building was completed. Accounts differ as to its fate after the new school was finished. Some think that it was remodeled into a home that stood on that corner. The president's home enjoyed a longer, useful life. It was moved behind the new school and was used by Superintendent Thomas Fuller as the school board offices. In the early 1920s, this building was remodeled as a dwelling for the new superintendent, Edwin Sanders Richardson. A new street was opened running north from College Street in front of the home. It was called Richardson Street in honor of the superintendent. Richardson continued to live in the dwelling until he resigned to become president of Louisiana Tech in 1936. The school board offices were relocated to the Webster Parish Courthouse (the 1905 structure). After Richardson left, the school board offices were relocated back into the former president's home. In the years after World War II, the school board offices were moved into the 1909 school building. In the summer of 1953, the old president's home was razed during the construction of the new Minden High School Building, still in use today. With the destruction of that home, the last building of the Minden Female College disappeared. However, one physical reminder of the Minden Female College is still present today, near its original site. The old bell that hung from a scaffold near the Concert

The buildings of the Minden Female College shortly before their demolition in 1910. The buildings were being used by the Minden Public School.

Hall is today the "Victory Bell" at Minden High School. The bell was sold to a junk dealer in 1953 when the 1909 Minden High School Building was destroyed. In 1964, under the leadership of MHS Student Council president Richard Campbell, the bell was rescued and returned to MHS, where it was mounted as it appears today.

Even though the buildings that composed the college disappeared, the legacy of learning and the memories of those families whose female members graduated from this pioneer school still survive. Descendants of the alumni of the Minden Female College have held prominent roles in the state of Louisiana during this century. Lizzie Murrell, of the class of 1875, married John T. Watkins, the son of John D. Watkins. John T. Watkins served as United States congressman from the Fourth District of Louisiana from 1903 until 1920. In 1920, he was defeated by John N. Sandlin, son of Irene McIntyre, of the class of 1857 and daughter of Dr. Alexander McIntyre, one of the original trustees of the college. Olive Goodwill, who attended the college during its later years, was the grandmother of Governor Mike Foster.

In 1933, Miss Ruth Reagan (later Mrs. Ruth Reagan Baird) compiled a list of living alumni of the Minden Female College during the Civil War era. They included Mrs. B.G. McIntyre of Minden; Mrs. Ellen C. Wren of Minden; Mrs. John Traylor of Minden; Mrs. John Shuttleworth of Shreveport; Mrs. Camille Bright Bell of Jackson, Tennessee (daughter of

Dr. J.E. Bright); Mrs. Dave Hadley of Minden; and Mrs. Ellen Mims of Minden. In 1954, Mrs. Thomas Campbell interviewed two living alumni of the school, Mrs. Nettie Holmes of the class of 1886 and Mrs. Dan Stewart Sr., for an article in the Minden newspaper.

In all probability, the students at Minden High School have no idea that they are attending classes on a site that has been used for education since 1838. They are also unaware that on that location was one of the pioneer institutions of higher learning in north Louisiana—a college that for nearly half a century produced graduates that became productive members of society and through the efforts of themselves and their descendants helped shape our lives in this region today. That institution, the Minden Female College, is one of the least understood and appreciated institutions of our local heritage. Truly, it created a legacy of quality education that remained in our city for decades after its doors closed for the final time.

CHAPTER 5

THE PRATT-LEWIS DUEL

This "Echo of Our Past" will center on one of the aspects of the old "Code of Honor" that has thankfully disappeared: dueling. Yet, more than just the story of a local duel of more than 130 years ago, this will be a story of two families that came to Minden from diverse locations, became a vital part of the community and were scarred by the tragic circumstances that developed as an outcome of that duel. The impact not only of the duel, but also of the families and their contributions to Minden, are part of the "Echo of Our Past."

Philomela Alden was born in Ashfield, Massachusetts, on December 10, 1783. Later she moved with her parents to western New York State, where at Williamstown she married Dr. Joel Rathbun on August 22, 1802. She and Joel had nine children, the last of which, also named Joel, was born in January 1821, five months after the death of his father, on August 20, 1820. Widowed with nine children, Philomela was eventually persuaded, in about 1835, to move south, to the area that is today Webster Parish, where three of her brothers had settled. Among the children accompanying Philomela was her twenty-year-old daughter, Dorliska. Dorliska Rathbun became a schoolteacher in the area of Minden and Overton.

About the same time as the Rathbuns moved to Louisiana, another emigrant from New England also arrived in our area. Luther Easton Pratt was born in Vermont in 1815. His family later settled in Massachusetts, where Luther received a quality fundamental education. He felt the urge to move west, so in 1835 he came south and settled in the village of Overton, just south of Minden along Bayou Dorcheat. He and Dorliska Rathbun became acquainted, and eventually romance developed and the couple was married in 1837 at Overton. Luther and Dorliska Pratt had eight children. Among these were Edward Eugene, who died at age twenty-three while in camp with the Minden Blues near Manassas, Virginia, in September 1861; Clarence Byron, who was the participant in the duel we will discuss; Daniel Webster, who served two terms as sheriff of Webster Parish; Laura Belle, who married Dr. Thomas Jefferson Vance of Minden and died here on August 26, 1933; and Alice Arimintha Pratt, who married William Alexander Sugg in 1874.

By the late 1840s, when John Langford Lewis came to Minden from Georgia, the Rathbuns and Pratts were already among the leading citizens of the community. Lewis also proved to soon be listed among the leaders of the local community in its political life. However, at this time few, if any, of the local residents knew of his background. Born in Georgia in 1807, he had studied law and been admitted to the bar. After his marriage to Martha Smith, he became very active politically in Muscogee County and particularly the city of Columbus, Georgia. Lewis served as an alderman and as mayor of Columbus as a very young man, and by 1841, he had become solicitor general of Muscogee County, an office that corresponds to the district attorney in our area. In 1842, during a very high-profile bank robbery case, Lewis was alleged to have received a portion of the money taken in the robbery in exchange for taking part in a scheme to allow the accused robbers to escape. Rather than stay and face charges, John L. Lewis moved west. He fought in the Mexican War and soon after came to Minden, hoping to leave his career in Georgia in the past. Lewis never practiced law here in Minden, and, in what may have been a plan to protect his assets from any outstanding claims, he made all property purchases in his wife's name. During the 1850s, although he didn't seek office, he became one of the leading figures in the Democratic Party in our area and in the state. He served as a delegate to the Democratic National Conventions in 1856 and 1860, and was an active opponent of secession. He was one of the Claiborne Parish delegates to the Louisiana Secession Convention of January 1861. Because of his views on the issues, he was named to the select committee that wrote the Louisiana Declaration of Secession, as it was felt that he would serve as a moderating influence on the language in that document.

Once the state approved the secession declaration, Lewis lined up with his state. He was the original commander of the Minden Blues and commanded the unit in the First Battle of Bull Run in the summer of 1861. That fall, he was a candidate for the Confederate Congress from our district and lost a disputed election to Henry Marshall of DeSoto Parish. Lewis had already gone to Richmond to take his seat in Congress when a recount declared Marshall the winner. Lewis reluctantly gave up the fight for a seat he thought he had won, and rather than return to the Blues, he came home to Minden.

Back in Minden, Lewis served several terms as mayor during the war. He entertained the leading Confederate officers, including French general Polignac, in his home, and was commissioned a colonel and placed in charge of recruiting the home guards for all of northwest Louisiana. Soon after the end of the war, Lewis had a sudden change in political affiliation. He joined the Republican Party and openly worked against his former friends and allies, who were fighting the forces of Reconstruction. With his previous political prominence, he became an important figure as military Reconstruction came to old Claiborne Parish. In 1868, he was appointed judge of Claiborne Parish. It is at this point that the stage for our duel is set.

One of the Confederate veterans returning to Minden at the end of the Civil War was Clarence Byron Pratt. Pratt had served under Lewis in the Minden Blues and was wounded at the Battle of Antietam in September 1862. After being furloughed home, he then enlisted in the First Louisiana Cavalry. While fighting with this unit, he was captured in the battles along the Rappahannock River on November 11, 1863. Pratt was sent to the Camp Morton, Indiana, where he remained a Federal prisoner until his parole on October 10, 1865. Pratt was held for so long after the end of the war because he refused to take the Oath of Allegiance to the United States. Once he took that oath, he was released.

Clarence Pratt returned to Minden as a young man of twenty-three, ready to resume his work as a printer that he had begun before the war. He also had developed a taste for politics and set out on a career in the public sector. Pratt and an associate established a local newspaper called the *Public Sentiment*, intended to express the opinions and ideas of the Confederate veterans and fight the forces of Reconstruction. In 1869, Clarence Pratt was elected to the Louisiana legislature from Minden and Claiborne Parish, at the age of twenty-seven. At about the same time, John Lewis gained his appointment as parish judge. In his dual capacity as editor and legislator, Pratt decided to do a little investigation of the mysterious background of John Lewis. After a little checking, he found the details of Lewis's public record back in Georgia. Pratt made that information public, not only in his newspaper, but also in a speech on the floor of the Louisiana legislature. The effect on Lewis was two-fold. Not only did he face the embarrassment of the long-ago charges of public bribery that he had never settled, but also, under the existing law passed by the same Congress that had impeached President

Andrew Johnson, he stood to lose his judgeship. The federal law said that anyone who had held a public office at any level prior to the Civil War, and then participated in the war on the side of the Confederacy, was ineligible to hold public office after the war. The rule didn't affect men such as Clarence Pratt, who had held no office before the war. So far as anyone in our area knew, it didn't affect John Lewis, as his first local office was mayor, and he took that office after secession. Pratt's revelation forced Lewis to be removed from the bench. In addition to revealing Lewis's past, Pratt had also made comments about the value of a man who turned his back on his friends and his cause as quickly as Lewis had in the wake of the war.

Publicly, Pratt was viewed as a hero, but understandably, the Lewis family had an entirely different view of the situation. Yet the Lewis family still had a good reputation and no one expected violence to become a problem. The wildcard in this situation was Robert Lewis, the youngest son of John and Martha Lewis. He felt that his family honor had been besmirched and he demanded satisfaction. Robert Lewis issued a challenge to Clarence Pratt to face him in a duel. Raised with the same sense of family and personal honor as Lewis, Pratt accepted the challenge without hesitation. A date was set and the duel was scheduled for the Pratt property at Overton. Future Louisiana Supreme Court justice Lynn B. Watkins served as Pratt's second in that duel. Details of the course of the duel are sketchy, but it is known that both men fired their weapons, although we have no record to indicate if the firing was simultaneous or one man fired first. Whatever the circumstances, Pratt's shot missed, but Lewis's bullet hit Pratt in the side. With his family's honor now satisfied, Lewis, in the strange sense of chivalry involved in dueling, provided his mattress so that the wounded Pratt could be carried back to Minden.

Although Pratt lived for five months after the duel, he eventually died from infection created by the bullet wound in December 1869 at the age of twenty-seven. The premature loss of such a talented young man is reflected in the obituary on his tombstone in the Minden Cemetery: "At morn the dew shall deck his grave, and shadow mantle it at noon, where lies the ever good and brave, whose hour of parting came too soon."

Robert Lewis would also meet a violent death. After the death of John Lewis, his children relocated to Red River Parish, where the oldest son of John and Martha Lewis, Will Lewis, had married and owned a plantation. In November 1881, Will Lewis died, leaving the management of his plantation and the care of their mother to his brother, Robert. Robert apparently expected this legacy to include the widow of Will Lewis. When Robert Lewis announced his love and his intentions to marry his sister-in-law on

Clarence Byron Pratt.

New Year's Eve 1881, she quickly turned him down and informed him that she and her sister would be leaving the plantation to live in New Orleans. Enraged, Lewis went to his room and then returned to his sister-in-law's room with a pistol and a knife. He shot and mortally wounded the sister-in-law who had rejected his affections, and also seriously wounded her sister. After this deed, Robert Lewis placed the pistol in his mouth and died at his own hand. The rashness that had sparked him to duel seemed to have also carried forward and brought an end to his own life.

Despite the tragic deaths of these two young men, the legacies of the two families are still seen here in Minden. The original land for the old Minden cemetery was given to the town by John and Martha Lewis, the very land where both Robert Lewis and Clarence Pratt are buried. As for the descendants of Luther and Dorliska Pratt, in addition to Daniel Webster Pratt serving as sheriff, descendants in families such as the Vance, Suggs and Wileys, among others, have taken leading roles in town. Clarence Wiley, a Pratt descendant, served for many years as clerk of court for Webster Parish. So not only does that duel in a field at Overton in 1869 give us a picture of the intense feelings generated during the years of Reconstruction, but one is also left to wonder what these young men could have achieved if not for that meeting that changed the course of both of their lives.

CHAPTER 6

WEBSTER PARISH: THE EDEN OF THE NEW SOUTH

By 1903, Minden and Webster Parish were experiencing growing pains, along with the rest of the nation. In 1893, at the Columbian Exposition in Chicago, Professor Frederick Jackson Turner had delivered his famous address outlining his "Frontier Thesis." In this speech, Turner declared that the frontier—as the United States had known it, the line between civilization and wilderness—had ceased to exist. He had commented on the need for a change in how the people of the United States viewed their society. One of the natural extensions of Turner's ideas came in 1920, when the United States Census reported for the first time that more than half of the people of the United States were urban residents, thus marking the first time that we were not a majority rural nation. These changes in society were being confronted by the leading citizens of Webster Parish in 1903, and they were alarmed. They recognized the symptoms of change in their community, particularly the dwindling number of farmers, and came up with what seemed a reasonable solution. A group was formed in Minden to determine how to attract more farmers to move to Webster Parish. This "Echo of Our Past" will examine that group formed over one hundred years ago, and how its members sought to respond to the changes in our community.

In April 1903, the Louisiana Land and Immigration Company was founded in Minden. F.H. Drake was chosen president, with Thomas Crichton as vice-president and Edmond L. Stewart, the man who started the idea for the organization, as secretary. The purpose of this company was to secure the listings of all available lands in Webster Parish with a view of selling them to immigrants, and to do any and everything to build up the country and save it from the collapse of farming. The group produced a small ten-page pamphlet that Stewart took to the Trans-Mississippi Conference in Seattle, Washington, in August 1903. He also placed these pamphlets in every train station he visited on his trip all the way north to St. Paul, Minnesota, and then all the way west to Seattle. This first distribution brought dozens of letters of inquiry and actually attracted a few settlers to the parish. One letter came from a man in Trion, Georgia, who reported that he knew of a great many farmers in his area who would be interested in relocating to Webster Parish. The company devoted substantial efforts to obtaining special concessions in the form of railroad rates, and several of the families were successful in making the move from Georgia to Webster Parish.

With these small successes to build upon, the Louisiana Land and Immigration Company set its sights on the St. Louis World's Fair of 1904 as the ideal place to promote Webster Parish. The Webster Parish Police Jury appropriated $350 to pay for the costs of printing a longer and more elaborate illustrated brochure to be distributed by the Louisiana State Board of Agriculture and Immigration at the St. Louis Fair. The jury's contribution was matched by a like contribution from the company. The leading railroad lines that connected to the Louisiana and Arkansas (L&A) line running through Minden and the Vicksburg, Shreveport and Pacific line through Sibley also bought advertisements in the booklet that helped defray the costs. I had the privilege of using a copy of that brochure through the courtesy of Mr. Frank Griffith, whose father, B.F. Griffith, was sheriff of Webster Parish in 1904. Let's see what those citizens of 1904 thought were the characteristics that would attract people to relocate to Webster Parish.

The brochure is titled *Webster Parish, Louisiana—The Homeseeker's Paradise—The Eden of the New South—The Promised Land of Peace and Plenty*. On the title page, since this information was geared toward farmers, was a listing of the crops that could be grown in Webster Parish, including peaches, plums, sugar cane, pears, figs, cotton, apples, grapes and corn. Following this were ads from the major railroads, showing how it was possible to make connections from areas north and east of Louisiana to Webster Parish. Also included were illustrations of Minden High School (then still housed in the old 1850s Minden Female College Building) and the plans for the soon-to-be-built 1905 Webster Parish Courthouse (which was torn down at the time the Minden Civic Center was constructed in 1969–70). Then the booklet began describing the reasons a farmer would want to settle in our parish.

The soil was described as easy to cultivate, and 90 percent of the land was considered cultivatable, requiring only "arousing to action with the plow

The 1905 Webster Parish Courthouse was built in the series of public improvements that went along with the campaign to promote immigration to Webster Parish.

and tickling with the hoe to make it laugh loudly with a rich harvest." The climate was described as moderate, with the temperature rarely reaching one hundred degrees, due to the "breezes from the Gulf of Mexico."

Winter snows were described as rare, with the earliest frost in middle October and the latest at the first of April. The claim was made of more days of sunshine in a year than in Italy, and that it is "never too warm or too cold to work out in the open air." (I guess they had forgotten five years earlier on February 13, 1899, when the temperature reached negative sixteen degrees in Minden. I hope no one worked outside that day.)

The parish was said to be crossed with ever-running springs of fresh water, including Indian Creek, Flat Lick, Cooley, Brushy, Black Lake, Sauceman, Sherman and Boone's Creek. Rolling and well-drained land was listed as the typical landscape. This drainage, and the elevation of three hundred feet, was said to contribute to the low death rate among the elderly and the children, the absence of yellow fever and the unusually "healthy, robust and energetic" citizens. The boast was made that "the parish officials, including the Clerk of Court, the Sheriff, the Assessor, the

Superintendent of Education, and the Parish Treasurer, all weigh over 200 pounds each." (As a person in the position to speak that mere weight is not a sign of health, I wonder how tall these healthy men were. More than 200 pounds on a person five and a half feet tall would not seem healthy.) The other men of the community were said to match these specimens, and the women were described as "healthy, pretty, intelligent and attractive as those of any other section of our Southland." Hospitality was considered as another major attraction of Webster Parish, as "worthy strangers are met with open-handed hospitality and given a cordial welcome."

Several pages were devoted to explaining the various crops that were being grown here and others that could be grown in Webster Parish. Cotton was listed as the staple crop, with yields of one-half to one bale per acre, with a current price of sixty dollars per bale. Other cash crops included corn, potatoes, oats, wheat, barley, rye, sorghum, sugar cane, tobacco, millet, alfalfa, peas, Bermuda grass, clover and all kinds of fruits, nuts and vegetables. While tobacco was listed among the crops, it was explained that none was currently being grown, but studies had indicated that it would grow in our soil. Cattle, hogs and horses were said to be able to live nine months on the native grasses and the remaining three months on oats, alfalfa and red clover.

The timber supply was said to have been thought until recently inexhaustible, but the many new mills were making inroads on the supply. Yellow pine was listed as the primary timber, with vast forests of oak, gum, cypress, hickory and beech. Bay, sassafras, ash, chinquapin, poplar, willow, maple, witch hazel, elm and mulberry were said to abound in the forest, while there was a more limited supply of walnut, locust and cedar.

Among the wildlife listed were wild deer, turkey, geese, ducks, squirrels, quail, snipe, trout, bass, perch, carp, buffalo and catfish. However, the brochure did warn that the supply of wildlife had been decreasing greatly since the years when a person could live year-round by the rod and the gun.

Business plans talked of an appropriation to erect a cotton factory at Minden, along with the idea of a trolley system. The booklet mentioned the recent construction of the railroad, cotton compress, oil mill and ice factory, brick factory, bottling works, foundry and other endeavors at Minden. Scattered throughout the book were pictures of some of the beautiful homes of Minden, some of which are still standing today.

Some needs were mentioned that an enterprising immigrant might want to invest in establishing. Minden had neither a laundry nor a dairy, and the brochure suggested that the market for either would be great. It was also

The City Park Gazebo. Both the park and the gazebo were also attempts to "spruce up" Minden.

suggested that a turpentine factory, a broom factory or a canning factory might be a success in the parish.

The availability of land was also a selling point to prospective new residents. The Bodcau Lumber Company at Minden and the Globe Lumber Company at Yellow Pine both had land for sale from $1.50 to $5.00 per acre. The parish tax rate was set at fifteen mills, while residents in Minden also paid an additional five mills for free public schools. The residents of each township in the parish paid a similar tax, and great attention was paid to the fact that all public schools in the parish were free and were being improved each year.

A selling point listed in the pamphlet was that no intoxicating liquors were allowed to be sold in the parish and anyone convicted of that offense was fined no less than $100. Another feature of the justice system was that all parish convicts were sentenced to work the roads, but the absence of crime caused a shortage of convicts, so all able-bodied males of age are required to work on the roads or pay for a proxy. Along the theme of the moral society, the many churches of the parish were described and pictures of the larger churches in Minden were also included.

The major industries of the parish were described in detail, along with testimonials from some of the earlier immigrants as to the success and

The 1909 Webster Parish Jail was given its "gothic" appearance as part of the campaign to modernize Minden.

happiness of their new lives in Webster. In conclusion, both to the pamphlet and to this article, here are the final fifteen reasons listed by the Louisiana Land and Immigration Company of Minden in 1904 in answer to the question of why settlers should want to come to our area.

Because it is the best country known for a man of moderate means.
Because you will find a country of rich soil awaiting the settler.
Because there are lands adapted to the growth of anything you plant.
Because you can be certain of profitable returns from whatever you put in the soil.
Because the winter does not consume what the summer produces.
Because there are more opportunities for diversified farming than anywhere else.
Because the seasons are regular, and no fear of crop failure.
Because the country is never scourged by cyclones and devastating storms or blizzards.

Because there is no better fruit country in the South: peaches, pears, plums, grapes, figs, besides other fruits and berries grow to perfection here.

Because truck farming is a success here: products being early on the market obtain high prices.

Because for healthfulness this section is unequalled on the face of the globe.

Because you have no long winter months to encounter, with no excessive dry heat in summer.

Because the climate is more uniform than most sections: no extremes of heat and cold.

Because you will find as orderly communities as anywhere on this continent.

Because you will find the most open-hearted people on the globe.

CHAPTER 7

MINDEN'S BRICK STREETS

One of the most recognizable landmarks of downtown Minden is Main Street with its bricks. We often like to mention Minden's brick streets, but as was recently pointed out to me by a relative newcomer, we now only have a single brick street. The bricks were, of course, removed from Broadway (or Back Street) during the 1970s, so the plural usage is now incorrect. In this "Echo" we will look at the history of the bricks on Main Street.

The brick paving of Minden's streets was part of a series of civic improvements carried out by the town government and local businessmen in the years between 1916 and 1918. The first step in this campaign was to have the downtown section of Minden curbed and guttered. The dirt streets in Minden had become a severe drainage problem. According to the *Webster Signal* of January 26, 1917, the Board of Aldermen of Minden first addressed the situation at its meeting of December 4, 1916. Aldermen at that time were J.S. Maxwell, Connell Fort, W.L. Winchester, George S. Carroll and W.C. Fields (not that W.C. Fields). Matt W. Lowe was serving as Minden's mayor. At that December meeting, the board authorized the Streets Committee, chaired by Connell Fort, to get estimates for curbing Main Street through the business district. In addition to this step, the board approved the construction of a concrete bridge over the branch on Pine Street "on the way to the bottling works" (just past the present intersection of College and Pine). Work progressed slowly on this project, as at the aldermen's meeting of February 5, 1917, the Streets Committee reported that estimates on the cost of the project were not yet complete. When the Board of Aldermen reconvened on March 5, the town attorney was instructed to draw up an ordinance to begin work on the curb and

A view of the dirt (mud) streets of the eastern end of downtown in the first decade of the twentieth century.

The heart of downtown Minden about 1909; notice the dirt streets and the wooden crosswalk in the foreground.

guttering process. However, public opinion among civic leaders was moving at a faster pace than the board's progress, and soon even more energetic planning for street improvement was underway.

The *Webster Signal* of April 6, 1917 (the same day that President Wilson delivered his message to Congress calling on the United States to enter World War I), contained two articles dealing with problems relating to the streets in Minden. The first was written by Editor Thomas W. Fuller of the *Signal*. Fuller called for stricter enforcement of the automobile speed limits in the town of Minden. He cited safety as a major reason, but also included among his arguments the problems created by dust. The passing of speeding cars through the dirt streets in the downtown area was causing excessive dust to be thrown on local businesses and shoppers. Fuller hoped that town leaders would respond to his complaints. Apparently, he had previously voiced this opinion to the proper sources because the same paper contained a warning from Town Marshal J.F. Maddry. The marshal announced a stricter enforcement of the speed limit, which was being ignored, particularly by "'jitney' operators and young men." Maddry reminded motorists that the speed limit in Minden was fifteen miles per hour, except in downtown, where it was eight miles per hour. Violators could expect to face charges.

On May 8, 1917, the Board of Aldermen made a formal call for bids to curb both sides of Main Street from Chaffe's Drugstore on the corner of Pine and Main eastward to Will Fuller's Garage, at the corner of Murrell and Main. When the curb and guttering process was completed, the street would be covered with Monroe gravel, donated to the town by Thomas Crichton. Even in those days, bureaucracy apparently slowed down public works. The bid opening, which was slated for May 23, did not actually occur until August 7, 1917.

In the interim, the problem of dust was becoming more and more severe. The dry weather of that summer was making the dust clouds in town a major nuisance. In the *Signal* of June 22, Fuller called for the town to purchase a street sprinkler to wet down the streets and prevent the clouds of dust that were such a health hazard.

Even as the street project lagged, the appearance of downtown Minden was beginning to change. The *Signal* of August 3 mentioned some of these changes. The new federal post office, valued at $50,000, was being completed at the corner of Main and Union (today's site of Hibernia Bank). This was Minden's first official post office building, as previously space had been rented by the post office department in private businesses.

Photographic image of the dirt streets looking east from the center of downtown, the intersection of Union and Main.

The United States Post Office on the corner of Union and Main, after the brick streets were constructed.

On the eastern end of downtown, W.R. Fogle had begun construction of a new Ford Garage on two vacant lots next to Chaffe's blacksmith shop. The building he erected would eventually serve as home to local Ford dealers from 1917 until 1972, and every Minden Ford dealer, including the present J.C. Johnson Ford, Inc., was at one time housed in that building. Today the location is the parking lot between Miller Woodard-Walker Insurance and the Tru Tone Hearing Aid Center. Next door to the Fogle Garage, Will T. Fuller had torn down his wooden garage and was building a concrete block structure that still occupies that corner today.

In other parts of downtown, Webb Hardware and Furniture was building a large new warehouse, which was only recently torn down, at West Union and Green Streets. On Broadway, adjacent to the town park, Joe R. Miller was renovating and modernizing his antebellum home. Today, the home still stands behind the Webster Parish Courthouse and was the home of Mr. Miller's daughter, Roy Miller Inabnett, until her death a few years ago. In addition to announcing all of these developments, that issue of the *Signal* also reported that the contract for curbing and guttering the streets of downtown had been awarded to the Rockbridge Construction Company of Shreveport.

In the spirit of progress, town leaders began to think of other improvements that could be made. A petition was circulated calling for a more drastic street improvement program. Since placing gravel on the streets would only be a temporary solution, this petition suggested that property owners be requested to pay for paving the street in front of their property from the curb to the middle of the street. The town would pay for the cost of paving the intersections, and the problem of quality streets would be solved for a much longer period. (Although I wonder if anyone expected the bricks to still be in use eighty-seven years later.)

In the *Signal* of September 4, 1917, local physician Dr. Luther Longino wrote a letter to the public. He proposed that now was the time for paving. The cost would never be lower. He felt that the only questions to be resolved were what type of surface should be used and how the paving should be funded. Longino felt that brick paving was the best answer, for, despite their high initial cost, the bricks would prove cheaper in the long run since they would last for years. (Perhaps Dr. Longino did expect them to be in use almost ninety years later.) He cited the support of local merchants and property owners to pay part of the costs. Additionally, he pointed out that by law, the city could go ahead and pave the streets and bill the property owners for two-thirds of the cost.

At its meeting on September 4, 1917, the Board of Aldermen received the petition from the citizens. It had been signed by over half of the property owners in the downtown area. In response, the board approved a resolution to receive bids for paving the section of Main Street that was currently being curbed and guttered. The new street would be constructed from paving bricks, placed on a "proper" foundation. This project moved forward much more quickly, spurred by public impetus. On October 2, 1917, bids were let on the project. The job was awarded to Kennedy & Olsen Construction of Kansas City, Missouri, the lowest of three bidders for the job. The specifications required paving bricks set in cement on a concrete foundation. Under the terms of the contract, the job was to begin immediately and was to be finished by January 1, 1918.

While the paving project was underway, civic-minded residents began another project to modernize downtown Minden. A committee was formed to secure street lighting for the newly constructed Main Street. The members of that committee were A.D. Turner, chairman; Arthur F. Dupuy, treasurer; and J.B. Flewellyn, A.M. Hough, A.B. Moreland and Dr. S.M. Richardson. In the *Signal* of November 17, the committee announced that adequate funds had been raised to purchase twenty lights and poles to place in the area from Fuller's Garage to Chaffe's Drugstore. Additional funds were to be raised to purchase poles and lights to cover the area from Chaffe's to the L&A Railroad Depot. Work was planned to begin immediately. As soon as sections of the street were paved, poles would be put into place. The lights and underground cable wiring would be installed as soon as the entire street was paved. The streetlights would be placed on alternate sides of the street, with the installation paid for by the town. After installation, the system would become town property.

Bad weather delayed the street paving beyond the original January 1, 1918 deadline. However, by February 15, 1918, work was nearing completion. On that night, another group of citizens approached the Board of Aldermen with a proposal. These citizens requested that funds be appropriated to continue the paving project from Pine Street to the L&A Depot. The leaders of this group were Dr. Longino, B.F. Griffith, J.R. Miller, W.R. Fogle, J.M. Miller, T.W. Fuller and W.B. Wiley. Citing the presence of the contractors in town with equipment and adequate supplies on hand, the men pleaded with the board to continue the project and allow another combination of public and private funding to pay the cost of continued construction. In a prophetic note, Longino, speaking for the committee, warned that if the town didn't take action now, it might well be

Looking east from the intersection of Pine and Main Streets, about 1907.

The same view, looking east from the intersection of Pine and Main Streets in the 1930s, with the brick streets.

years before any other steps would be taken to improve local streets. The board appointed a committee to study the plan.

While that paving project was being considered, on the other end of downtown, another extension was requested. Representatives of the First Methodist Church, upon seeing how well Kennedy & Olsen had done the job in the rest of downtown, came before the Board of Aldermen and requested that the bricks be extended for another block, paving the area in front of the church and its parsonage. The city was unable to fund this request but a compromise was reached between the town and the church, with the assistance of the Crichton family, which also owned property in that block. The city agreed that if the church would allow the extension of the street to be made on gravel, rather than concrete, the plan would be considered. The Crichton family agreed to provide the gravel for the base and the church accepted the modified plan. Two-thirds of the cost of this extension was paid by the city, while the church paid for the other third. So from 1918 until the bricks were removed and put back into place during the 1990s, that one block of downtown was on a gravel foundation, rather than a concrete base.

By May of 1918, no action had been taken on the request to extend the bricks to the L&A Depot. Two events in that month killed the chances of that ever happening. First, the contractors removed the equipment, as the city had shown no inclination to moving ahead with the added paving. The second event came on the evening of May 25, 1918, when a devastating fire destroyed Minden's largest industry, the Minden Lumber Mill of the Bodcau Lumber Company. For the next few years, Minden's economy languished and few civic improvements were undertaken. Perhaps the only one of any note was the construction of the town power plant to provide electricity for Minden. Prior to the fire, the power plant of the Minden Mill had also provided electricity for the town. After the mill was destroyed, Minden was literally "in the dark" for part of that summer of 1918 until an emergency power apparatus could be set up in August 1918. The notion to pave Main Street to the depot was never fulfilled. Proving Dr. Longino's prediction true, no further bricks were added to Minden's streets for nearly seven years. Finally, in 1925, brick streets were added to Broadway (Back Street), but by then it was felt that placing paving bricks all the way to the depot was no longer practical. So the era of building brick streets in Minden ended.

For the next fifty years, Minden retained its two brick streets. However, on July 9, 1975, the bricks on Broadway were removed as part of what the *Minden Press-Herald* called the "brick street compromise." When Mayor Pat

The bicentennial gazebo erected in Jacqueline Park in 1976 and constructed of the bricks removed from Broadway.

Patterson first announced that plans were being made to overlay Broadway, city hall was bombarded with complaints that the bricks should not be covered up. So, in a compromise, Patterson and Streets and Parks commissioner Jack Batton announced that the bricks would be removed, cleaned and stored. A short time later, plans were made to construct a bandstand or gazebo in Jacqueline Park to somewhat replace the much beloved wooden bandstand that stood in City Park from 1908 until the construction of the Webster Parish Courthouse on its present site in 1952. The bricks from Broadway were used to build the present gazebo and the brick sidewalks and flowerbeds in Jacqueline Park as part of a project celebrating our nation's bicentennial. So that's the story of one of the first things mentioned in any discussion of downtown Minden, the brick street.

CHAPTER 8

E.S. RICHARDSON

Most residents of Minden are familiar with the name E.S. Richardson as the elementary school next to Turner's Pond. But few remember the man the school was named for, a man who almost single-handedly brought education in Webster Parish into the twentieth century. This "Echo of the Past" is about E.S. Richardson and how his actions of more than seventy years ago still reverberate in our community today.

Edwin Sanders Richardson was the second child born to James Sanders Richardson and Sallie Havis Richardson, on August 31, 1875. (Edwin's younger brother, Samuel Milton Richardson, born on January 5, 1878, would become a well-respected doctor in Minden, as would Samuel Milton's two sons, Samuel Milton Jr. and Thomas.) E.S. Richardson was reared in Claiborne Parish, and attended the Eureka School in Langston, where his father was the teacher. In addition, Edwin studied one summer under T.H. Harris, later the Louisiana state superintendent of education. Upon finishing all the education available to him in Claiborne Parish, young E.S. Richardson took jobs teaching in one-room schools in Claiborne and Webster Parish for thirty dollars per month. He saved this money and was able to attend George Peabody College for Teachers in Nashville, Tennessee. In 1900, he was awarded a licentiate of instruction from Peabody. Although he never returned to school as a regular student, Peabody awarded him a BA degree in 1935. He also received an honorary doctor of laws from Centenary College in 1938.

From 1900 to 1904, he served as principal of the Atlanta, Arkansas high school. While he was there, a new school building was built, an omen of things to come in his career. Richardson was offered a lifetime contract by the school's Board of Trustees, but in 1904, he was given an opportunity to return home to Louisiana as a teacher at Saline School in Bienville Parish, and he left the Arkansas job.

During the next four years, he worked in the Bienville Parish school system, first at Saline, later at Liberty Hill School and finally as teacher and principal at Bienville High School, where once again he supervised the construction of a new building. Shortly after the Bienville building was completed, Richardson was named superintendent of schools of Bienville Parish, a position he held until 1911.

Professor C.A. Ives hired E.S. Richardson to work in the Agricultural Extension Department of the Louisiana State University in 1911. The years he spent in that post shaped Richardson's philosophy of education. His writings from those years show that he was already sketching out plans for school consolidation, agricultural education, vocational training and centralized control, ideas he would later implement in Webster Parish. One notation in 1917 outlines a consolidation campaign nearly identical to the one he conducted in Webster Parish years later. During his years in the extension office, Richardson became best known for his use of audiovisual equipment. He used trucks that had projectors built onto the truck bed, enabling him to go to farmers in the rural areas and show films on the latest techniques in farming.

In 1919, Richardson was named superintendent of Webster Parish schools, a job that became the crowning achievement of his career as an educator. With the strong backing of School Board president W.G. Stewart, Richardson transformed the Webster Parish schools into a model system copied by counties throughout the country.

When Richardson took over in Webster Parish, there were thirty-nine schools in the parish, thirty-five of which were one- to three-room schools. There were only four certified high schools in the parish. In the white schools of Webster Parish there were one hundred teachers: eighteen held BA degrees; thirty-two others had two years of college and a teaching certificate; forty-six had passed an examination and met no formal education requirement; and nine had not even passed the examination. The only black school operated by the parish was a small building in Minden. (There were some other black schools operated by churches.)

Richardson hit the ground running in his new post. His routine included nearly daily visits into the schools, personal evaluations of the teachers and contact with parents and civic leaders. He began a public relations blitz to support a consolidation campaign by persuading the rural residents that the educational opportunities for their children would be much greater in a

E.S. Richardson examining books during the opening of the Webster Parish Library in 1929.

The Gum Springs School west of Minden, typical of the rundown, one-room schools Richardson found in Webster Parish.

larger school. Richardson's consolidation campaign was a smashing success. By 1925, ten centralized, state-approved high schools were built. These were located in Shongaloo, Evergreen, Minden, Dubberly, Heflin, Springhill, Sarepta, Cotton Valley, Doyline and Sibley. By 1928, each of these schools had new buildings and all except Evergreen's were brick. Twenty-four small schools were abandoned and only seven small schools remained. Richardson contracted with the W.H. Luck Company of Minden to build bodies for forty "school trucks," or buses, to bring the rural children into the larger schools that offered a broader curriculum.

By 1931, the remaining seven small schools were closed and Richardson had completed implementation of the County Unit system, a uniform, parish-wide system of purchasing with a centralized warehouse. Books, equipment and supplies were purchased by the parish and standardized in all schools. If a school needed a new desk, or additional books, instead of having to find an outside source, it merely contacted the central warehouse in Minden. A uniform salary schedule for teachers, based on education and experience, was adopted. By the time Richardson left Webster Parish in

The new 1924 Minden High School building, which was the new home for area students from the outlying campuses like Gum Springs.

1936, the white schools had 127 teachers: 4 held MA degrees; 65 held BAs; 30 had three years of college; 26 had completed two years of college; 1 had one year of college; and only 1 teacher had less than one year of college training.

In 1922, Richardson succeeded in passing a bond issue to build the Webster Training School for black students and to hire a supervisor for black schools. Through the Rosenwald Fund and other sources, Webster Parish opened thirty-five black schools, and by 1932 the Webster Training Institute had five buildings and expanded course offerings.

Not forgetting his agricultural background, Richardson also created canning kitchens and meat-processing plants at rural schools and arranged for students to participate in soil erosion projects being conducted in the area.

Richardson was also instrumental in obtaining Rosenwald funding to set up the new Webster Parish Library in 1929 to serve both black and white residents. Richardson served on the first parish Library Board. The School Board hired eleven teacher librarians and allowed the branch libraries to be placed in the schools during the school year, in addition to financially supporting the library system.

Richardson's achievements and the improved school system in Webster Parish did not escape local, statewide and even nationwide notice. He was

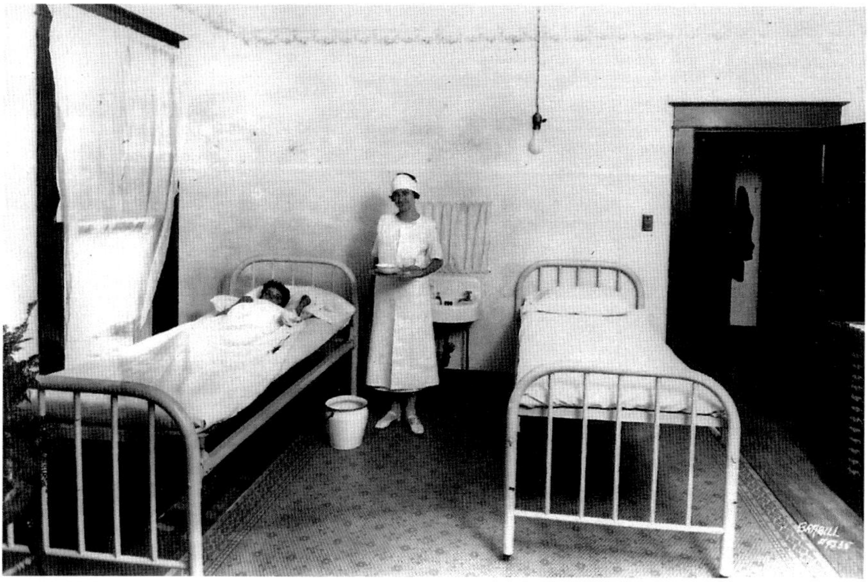

The infirmary at the 1924 Minden High School.

in great demand to speak at conferences nationwide on his County Unit system, which was seen as the answer to many problems of rural school districts where individual communities couldn't support adequate schools. In the late 1920s, the Webster Parish School Board raised Richardson's salary to $5,000 per year, over the state-allowed maximum of $4,000, and the board went to the State Supreme Court to assure that Richardson received the well-deserved raise. In 1927, the State Association of School Administrators held a three-day meeting in Minden to study the Webster Parish system as a model, and educators from various parts of the nation came on a regular basis to observe the Webster Parish schools as a pattern for their own districts.

Such achievements made it inevitable that Richardson's career advanced, and in 1936, he was named president of Louisiana Tech. His tenure at Tech was cut short in 1941, when the Sam Jones administration purged all administrators appointed during the years of Huey Long's control.

After leaving Tech, Richardson returned to Minden, where he served as executive secretary of the Webster Council, coordinating activities between federal and parish agencies involved in the construction of the new Louisiana Ordnance Plant. Later, as a housing shortage emerged, he accepted the position as federal rent director for the Minden area. His final position of public service was as a field representative for the State Department of

One of the Luck school buses that allowed Webster Parish to be a pioneer in transporting students to school.

E.S. Richardson Elementary School in Minden, named for Superintendent Richardson.

Commerce and Industry under Governor Jimmie Davis. Richardson retired and moved back to Ruston in 1948, where he died on October 11, 1950.

So now you know that E.S. Richardson is more than the school by Turner's Pond—you know that he was a man with a vision who helped make our schools some of the best in the nation.

CHAPTER 9

MARDI GRAS 1923

The tradition of celebrating Mardi Gras began in Minden after the Civil War, about the time the celebration became so large in New Orleans. By the early years of the twentieth century, the celebration of Mardi Gras was a special occasion in Minden. Beginning about 1902, the festivities grew in size each year until February 13, 1923, when one of the worst tragedies in the history of our town occurred during a Mardi Gras celebration. This "Echo of our Past" examines the history of Mardi Gras in Minden, with a focus on the Mardi Gras fire of 1923 that brought an end to the first era of large-scale celebration of Fat Tuesday in our town.

Although there are surviving images of local celebrations from the late nineteenth century, one of the first written references to the local Mardi Gras celebrations dates from Friday, February 14, 1902, when the *Webster Signal* carried the following account: "Tuesday was Mardi Gras day and the very spirit of carnival gaieties extended far and near. The street pageants were more gorgeous than ever and the balls were brilliant social events."

Each year the celebration grew, as photos show the parades with the royalty wearing gowns and formal wear traveling through downtown in open cars, while wagons and trucks were used as crude floats. Events were scheduled for all ages, and the parades were always staged on the actual day of Fat Tuesday. The schools were dismissed for the day, as the festivities included a day full of fun and games for the children.

On Friday, February 16, 1917, the *Webster Signal* reported:

> *Mardi Gras will be celebrated next Tuesday beginning with a grand parade at 2:30. Everybody is invited to take part and join in the parade. The Civic*

> *Clubs offer two prizes of $2.50 each for the best decorated automobile and vehicle consisting of carriage, buggy, wagon, etc.*
>
> *An evening entertainment will be given at the picture show consisting of crowning the queen and several very enjoyable numbers of home talent as well as a choice 4-reel picture will be presented. The entertainment will begin at 7:30—35 cents for grown-ups and 15 cents for children. The parade is to be formed near the compress. Everybody cordially invited to join in the parade and don't forget the evening's entertainment at 7:30 at the picture show.*

On Thursday, February 10, 1921, the *Webster Signal* announced: "The high school has combined Mardi Gras queen with Valentine queen to be held February 14th at Minden High School."

Also in 1921, the following account appeared in the *Webster Signal*:

> *Mardi Gras has always been an occasion of much festivities in Minden, but seldom has more enthusiasm and true enjoyment been exhibited than on this year. The old and young alike took part in the masking, making the afternoon and evening affairs much more spectacular. Never before has there been such a variety of costumes for knights and ladies and natives of every country were there in plenty. Little children of every size and age contributed to the spirit of the day and were extremely happy in their bright colored effective costumes. The afternoon from 3 to 5 o'clock was their time. On account of the rain it was impossible to have the parade. However, the crowd gathered in the American Legion Hall where an excellent program was rendered.* [At that time, the American Legion Hall was the third floor of the Crichton Hardware Building; the current American Legion Home was not built until 1950.] *It was there that the lovely little Queen and her chosen King were crowned with all due honor and dignity. The throne was most attractive indeed, in all the regal tapestry and canopy. It was there that Mary Lewis Fort, as the most popular little girl, was crowned Queen of the younger set and Elliot Howe was crowned King.*
>
> *Roy Miller* [later Mrs. J. Lenwood Inabnett] *and Nancy Belle Lee, ladies-in-waiting, escorted by the knights of the court—Minden Fitzgerald and Clarence Wiley* [who later served as Webster Parish clerk of court for many years]. *Page was Wilbur Lowe, Crown-bearer was Ethel Moore. A dance was performed by Gwendolyn Youngblood, while Tom Glass was a clown; Connell Dupuy, James Reagan and Ben Wiley*

contributed a minstrel act. Ivan Lowe and Zoulana Barnett came as Maggie and Jiggs, followed by a grand march and refreshments. Proceeds went to the Civic Clubs.

Evening program was a combination program and a dance. Queen was Miss Beatrice Lee, Daughter of Mrs. J.B. Lee. [In later years, she married Eugene Houston and moved to Bossier City. Her son was the late country music star David Houston.] *The King was Eddie Bryan* [the husband of Mrs. Elsie Bryan and the father of Mrs. Jo Ann McKinney], *son of Mr. and Mrs. W.T. Bryan* [he was chosen by the queen]. *Their attendants were: Mabel Life and H.L. Bridges; Maurice Barnes and Julian Means; Katherine Lunsford and Louie Bryan. Little James Nelson sang "Hail to the King and Queen." James Knighton served as Jester and Wilbur Lowe was the crown bearer.*

The band was composed of J.N. Koch, Leland Mims (longtime Webster Parish police juror), Courtland Murph and Earl Looney, who later gained international fame as an artist. Miss Esther Evans (later daughter-in-law of Congressman John N. Sandlin) gave readings entitled "Just a Wearying for You" and "French Doll." Miss Gladys Durham's dance pupils—Sybil Winn, Nina Wiley, Olive Roberts, Dorothy Goodwill, Treeby Miller and Maud Dickens—performed interpretive dance. (Please notice the name Olive Roberts, who was the mother of former governor Mike Foster. Treeby Miller was the mother of Thad Andress.) Mrs. Walter Webb Jr. (postmistress of Minden), who was dressed as an Irish lassie, and Attorney W.W. McDonald, dressed as winter, won the best costumes. After expenses, the Civic Club donated the proceeds to the starving children of Europe.

In 1922, Mardi Gras was observed on Tuesday, February 28. Those attending in the three- to six-year-old section were Miss Martha McDade, queen; Mr. Harry McInnis, king; knights were Aubrey Hough and Wilkins McDade; Rollin Williams Jr. was crown bearer; Thomas Crichton Jr. and McVoy McIntyre were train bearers; Rolene Rathbun (later Mrs. Davidson Brown, who taught English at Minden High School for many years) and Jane Goodwill were maids; Horace Thomasson was jester; and Ernest Smith was the herald.

The program was as following: crowning of the queen and an orchestra selection, followed by a dance by Louise Denmon. There was a balloon dance by Rolene Rathbun, Mable Ruth Coombs, Jane Goodwill and Jamie Garrison. The Blue Bird Dance was performed by Onie Stephens, Virginia

Bullock, Virginia Miles, Nancy Belle Lee, Roy Miller (Mrs. Inabnett), Pauline Dickens, Ruth Reagan, Ida B. Mixon and Leila Sandefur.

There were sketches from childhood, with the artist Helen Nelson. The following children acted the parts of the five senses: Sight, Grace Virginia Rathbun; Touch, David Williams; Smell, Ann Howe; Taste, Jimmie Chaffe; Hearing, Sallie Hutton (later the wife of Dr. C.S. Sentell). A chorus sang "Ain't We Got Fun." A dance ensued. That evening, King James Davis and Queen Maude Dickens were crowned. Lords and ladies were Burgess White and Dorothy Goodwill, and Earl Looney and Treeby Miller. Crown bearer was Robert Semmes Webb; train bearers were Jack Connell (local dentist for many years) and Laura Harkness; jester was Horace Thomasson; herald was Ernest Smith. The program consisted of a selection by the Beer Bottle Band, trained to play the bottle by Mrs. J.B. Snell (Ada Jack Carver) and led by Elliot Howe. The Gypsy Trail was a dance and song in costume by Gladys Durham, Helen Brown, Jessie Mae Sullivan, Marjorie Ogden, Susanella Schoenbrodt (who taught elementary grades in Minden for over thirty years), Valrae Farrar (Mrs. N.C. Strange), Jacqueline Taylor (Mrs. Will Davis), Miriam Fuller and Ruth Mims.

Also, Miss Mabel Hickman (who lost her life the following year, in 1923, in the fire at the Mardi Gras program) gave a reading. A minstrel comedy was performed by Charles Dutton, Wood Brown, Robert Watkins (later city judge), John Fort (who ran the local newsstand for so many years), Mack Dunlap and H.L. Bridges (son of one of Minden's mayors). The Glow Worm Dance line included Lilla Stewart, Ruby McDonald, Eugenie Burt (another casualty of the fire the next year at the Mardi Gras program), Mary Em Phillips, Georgia Howe and Nell Gray. There was a piano selection by Mrs. L.H. Denmon and an Irish song and dance by Ruth Mims, along with "History of the Dance" by Mabel Winn and Dan Stewart (later a local attorney). Miss Zenia Fuller and Lillian McCoy, in gypsy costumes, had a fortunetelling tent. The Civic Club committee was composed of Mrs. R.A. Baker, Mrs. Donald Goodwill, Mrs. Felix Drake Jr., Mrs. A.D. Turner, Mrs. Joe R. Miller, Mrs. W.B. Wiley and Mrs. P.A. Rathbun. The Civic Club received the proceeds from this event.

But the Mardi Gras event of 1923 was not the happy occasion it had been in prior years; rather, it was the cause of sadness and mourning here in Minden for many years. The *Bossier Banner* (Minden papers for the time from November 1922 through May 1923 were lost) of February 15, 1923, carried the following account of the tragedy:

School buses outside the 1910 Minden High School building, the only brick building that Richardson "inherited" when he became superintendent of schools for Webster Parish.

> *Keenest regret is felt here in Benton because of a tragedy of the week occurring in Minden. Tuesday night eight young ladies of that place who were taking part in a Mardi Gras play, and a little girl of eight years who was behind the scenery on the stage, were severely burned and four of them have since died. The dead are Miss Dorothy Cheshire, a daughter of Mrs. Dolly Cheshire, a former resident of North Bossier, Miss Eugenie Burt, Miss Mabel Hickman, ranging in age from sixteen to seventeen years in age, and the little girl who was mentioned above, Eva Eleanor Lowe, whose clothes were ignited as the older girls ran by her. The names of the others burned are: Miss Ruth Reagan* [we know her as Mrs. Ruth Reagan Baird, who gave so many years of service at the Webster Parish Library], *Miss Vashti Bullock, Miss Vallye Watson, Miss Alma Sullivan and Miss Eloise Hough, aged from fifteen to seventeen years. The fire originated when the dress of Miss Alma Sullivan caught fire from a sparkler, which was being used to enhance the effect of a snow scene in the culminating act of a snow scene of a Mardi Gras play. The other girls ran to the assistance of their companion and their dresses caught fire from the flames of her dress. The play was being held in the Minden High School auditorium under the auspices of Civic Clubs of Minden. The girls ran from a single exit trying to escape the flames. The wind, as they ran, fanned the flames. Their dresses were of flimsy material, bearing specks of cotton in imitation of snow. Young men ran after the girls and tried to extinguish the flames. However they were all badly burned and others are expected to die.*

The participants in the Minden Mardi Gras pageant of 1923, in a photo taken at the afternoon rehearsal before the deadly fire.

Another girl later succumbed to burns received that night, bringing the total number of dead to five.

This fire took place in the 1910 high school building that was on the site of the present Minden High School. Sorrow stunned our community. Witnesses described seeing the balls of fire outside the window of the auditorium but did not know that it was the girls with their dresses aflame. The next morning, people were gathered in groups of twos and threes all along the streets, each group talking over the events that caused such sadness in Minden. Mrs. Lenwood Inabnett was there that night. She has said that they had daubed the cotton with black shoe polish to make it look like ermine. That shoe polish made the fire even more volatile. Those who were burned but lived bore the terrible burn scars for the remainder of their lives. The memories are still vivid with those who were here at that time.

The picture that accompanies this article was made available to me by Cynthia Garrison Payne, who inherited it from her aunt, Jamie Craton Garrison. Jamie Garrison was a participant in the pageant in 1923, and this picture shows the cast of the pageant in an image taken on the afternoon of February 13, 1923, just prior to the fire.

In aftermath of this tragedy, Mardi Gras celebrations in Minden came to a complete halt for a few years. On the first anniversary of the fire, the local paper carried no mention of Mardi Gras celebrations—only a poem dedicated to the memory of those who had perished on February 13, 1923. Later, smaller-scale celebrations were held, but World War II brought an end to local Mardi Gras celebrations until the very recent past. So while our history does have many happy memories of past Mardi Gras celebrations, there is one poignant, haunting "Echo of Our Past" from Mardi Gras 1923.

CHAPTER 10

THE 1933 TORNADO

Monday, May 1, 1933, dawned like most spring days in north Louisiana. The air was pleasant, but one detected a hint of the heat and humidity characteristic of a Louisiana summer already creeping into the atmosphere. The initial shock of the bank failure had passed, and Mindenites were beginning to adapt to the changes. The most excited residents on that day were schoolchildren happily starting the last week of an abbreviated school year. The school year had been shortened by two weeks just before Christmas 1932 because of an influenza attack and had remained closed the first two weeks of January 1933 because funding from the state had not been received. But the year did not seem shorter to the children, because to make up for lost days, school had been held in six-day sessions since January. So, as the last week of school began, excitement centered on "free" Saturdays, summer and the high school graduation scheduled for the following Friday, May 5.

During the day, a typical spring thunderstorm system began moving through northwest Louisiana. About 4:00 p.m., this line of storms drew near to Minden, approaching like most dangerous weather systems in north Louisiana, from the southwest. This was not a typical storm system, however. Just northwest of Minden, the line of storms spawned a massive tornado that soon vented its fury upon Minden. The approaching storm caused little alarm in Minden, since the town had not been threatened by turbulent weather during the 1930s. No formal tornado watch or warning was issued by the National Weather Service, and the storm seemed as normal as any other spring thunderstorm. In fact, while residents of northeastern Minden wondered if Shreveport was "getting a rain" out of the cloud to the west, residents of Bayou Avenue on the northwestern side of town were already

A home destroyed on South Broadway by the tornado of May 1, 1933.

feeling the storm's power. The funnel cloud first touched down on Bayou Avenue in an area adjacent to the railroad tracks and near the railroad yard. It struck with great intensity, and several fatalities, including three members of one family, were registered in this area. The tornado moved southward and began to lift up, destroying homes on Winchester Hill, located just west of the railroad yard. A traveling salesman eating at the Highway Café at the foot of Winchester Hill on the Shreveport highway heard the storm approaching. He ran to his car and immediately fled the area, driving to Shreveport. Once he arrived there, he relayed the first reports of the destructive nature of the tornado to Shreveporters and started the flow of assistance from the Shreveport area.

The storm then turned to the east and touched down on the northern side of North Broadway, just beyond the headquarters building of the Louisiana and Arkansas Railroad, leaving in its wake thousands of dollars of damage in the industrial and commercial area along the railroad tracks. Several houses on the slope of the hill leading to the downtown area were destroyed, including one house where a birthday party was being held for a ten-year-old girl. The honoree and some of the guests at this party were killed. The funnel

A scene of destruction in the Minden Cemetery after the tornado.

The severely damaged headquarters building of the Louisiana and Arkansas Railroad in the aftermath of the May 1, 1933 tornado.

Looking west on Broadway at the wreckage of St. Ann's Catholic Church after the tornado.

cloud lifted again, toppling the newly dedicated Confederate statue located in the park formed by the median between North and South Broadway on the hillside. The only damage to the statue was a broken end to the soldier's bayonet, but the rest of Minden would not fare as well. In addition, it was during this phase of the storm that the Minden Cemetery, on the opposite side of the hill from the L&A headquarters, was devastated by the storm.

Continuing toward the east, the storm drew nearer to downtown, destroying the St. Anne's Catholic Church on South Broadway. At that point, the killer funnel made another change in course, veering toward the south. This direction change spared downtown Minden from major destruction. However, this new course caused the most severe damage, in terms of human lives, during the storm's devastating trip through the Webster Parish center. The funnel cloud turned just in time to miss the antebellum home of Joe Miller. Instead, it vented its full force on the rental property known as the Miller Quarters, located directly behind the Miller home. Over eighty rental houses owned by Joe Miller were destroyed and their residents left homeless. That entire neighborhood of Minden's black community had seen its world blown away. The tornado continued to the southeast, following Maiden Lane, which bisected Minden's black community, smashing houses on both sides, flattening the area like an exploded bomb. The storm passed completely through Minden's black community and spiraled up again at the Webster Training Institute, the black high school, on Highway 80 East. At that point, the funnel lifted into the heavens, leaving behind a stunned Minden to assess its damage and begin recovery. The storm system continued to the east, and later in the day, farm workers in Marion, Louisiana, seventy miles to the northeast, were showered with papers from the Webster Training Institute, and residents of Vienna, Louisiana, found American history exams from Minden High School.

Minden was in a state of chaos, from physical destruction and from bewilderment over the nature of the storm itself. No living resident could remember experiencing a tornado in Minden. Alberta Glass, who had resided in Minden since 1867, recalled such a storm north of the town about 1910, but said no tornado had ever touched down in the immediate vicinity of Minden. My father's family stood on the porch of their home watching the storm's approach. They did not realize the danger or try to flee until after the tornado had lifted their home off its supporting blocks and set it back into place. My father remembered seeing a cow lifted by the storm carried past them, much like Dorothy in *The Wizard of Oz*.

Stories of near-death and unique occurrences were told after the storm. The office employees of the Minden Cotton Oil and Ice Company, located near the railroad tracks, were saved by taking shelter in a drainage culvert underneath the railroad tracks. Many citizens reported seeing cows, chickens and other animals being carried by the funnel cloud. Others described entire houses sailing by or pine needles embedded into telephone poles. Sam Life encountered a brush with death. He was standing in front of Parker's Garage on the Dixie-Overland Highway (U.S. 80) when a tornadic gust of wind lifted him into the air. Life was transported by the storm over one hundred yards and deposited in the yard of Mrs. Webb, unharmed but quite naturally shaken.

In preparation for this story, I asked for my readers to submit their tornado memories, and I received three stories that I will now relate.

Rae Lumpkin Ratcliff was a young Minden High School graduate living on her father's dairy farm located just south of Minden (today well within the city limits, but this was 1933). As the skies darkened and the storm approached, her father called the entire family to go into the root cellar. When the storm cleared, she and her siblings came out and saw all the debris in the air and covering the landscape coming from the nearly complete destruction of the local black residential community. Her mother was attending a Women's Missionary Union (WMU) meeting at First Baptist

Looking east toward the intersection of Pine and Main Streets in the aftermath of the tornado.

Church on that Tuesday afternoon. The ladies, of course, did hear a storm, but really weren't aware that anything significant had happened until they came outside and saw the damage.

Frank Griffith was a small boy living in his family home (where he still resides today) on Elm Street. Frank remembers sitting in the kitchen looking out the back windows of his house when the storm appeared, and it seemed to be coming right at their home. It appeared to Frank and his father, former sheriff B.F. Griffith, that the storm was so close that it was about to destroy the fences at the back of their property, when suddenly they saw the storm make its large turn to the east. It was only then that they realized that the storm had not been so close; it was merely the size of the funnel that caused that illusion. Sheriff Griffith, Frank and his mother loaded into the car and went to check on a relative who lived on McDonald Street. The relative was safe, so Frank and his dad then went downtown. They got as far as Tom Glass's store, located on the southeast corner of Main and Union Streets (today the site of the Community Hospice of America, but better known to many older residents as the second home of the old People's Bank and

The severe damage and destruction in the Maiden Lane area of Minden looking toward the wrecked Sibley Road Gin and the Minden Cotton Compress.

Trust). Frank remembers that the windows had been completely blown out of the store and the glass was all over the sidewalk. In his hurry to see the damage, Mr. Griffith hadn't noticed that Frank was barefooted. When someone pointed out that the little boy was standing barefoot in the glass, Mr. Griffith chided Frank.

Eunice Hart of Minden related a story told her by a coworker at the Louisiana Army Ammunition Plant, a Mrs. Parker, who was reared in Haughton and was about twelve years old at the time of the storm. Mrs. Parker's mother had died and she lived with her father. On that afternoon, they were coming to Minden to do some business and reached the outskirts of downtown just as the storm had passed. As her father started up Depot Hill, he soon saw that there were literally storm victims lying on the ground. He had trained his daughter to drive the truck at her young age to help with chores on the farm, and he told her to get into the driver's seat. While the young girl drove the vehicle, the father found those victims still living, loaded several into the back of his truck and took them to get medical attention.

In the storm's wake, other citizens of Minden were not so fortunate; the tornado claimed twenty-eight lives in Minden. Well over one hundred other people were injured. The devastation was so great in the black community that an approximate death total was not obtained for several days, and no precise accounting of injuries to black residents was ever made. The severity of the storm damage in this part of Minden caused early wire service accounts carried in Tuesday morning papers, such as the *New York Times*, to estimate the death toll at eighty. Crews of volunteers aided by local Boy Scout troops combed the rubble for two days after the storm looking for additional bodies. The newspapers, in the months after the storm, continued to list deaths caused by storm injuries. Because of the way deaths were handled in the black community, we will probably never know the true loss of life in that storm.

Beyond the human loss, actual physical damage to property was staggering. Damage estimates placed the total loss at about $1,250,000. There were 310 homes and businesses destroyed, 217 of which were in the black community. A crew of three hundred men worked for five days just to clear all the streets of debris. Their efforts were greatly hindered by a rush of sightseers from nearby towns. Over thirty thousand people came to view the storm damage within two days following the storm. The congestion became such a problem that mayors and newspaper editors of nearby towns asked their citizens to please refrain from traveling to Minden and police roadblocks were set up to stop all traffic entering Minden, except the ones engaged in official business.

The first step Mindenites made toward recovery was to provide for the homeless. George E. Myer, director of the Red Cross Relief Project, reported that 1,200 people were left homeless by the storm (about 20 percent of the population of Minden). The vast majority of these were black residents. Refugee camps for the homeless were established at the parish training school on the east side of town and in boxcars at the railroad yard on the west side of Minden. An emergency hospital was placed in the parish armory to help care for the injured in the black community. Dr. W.C. Sumner, parish health officer, set up an inoculation program to avoid outbreaks of disease in the refugee camps. Other relief projects were set up with funds collected by community drives in northwest Louisiana. About $70,000 would eventually be sent to Minden to aid in recovery from the tornado. A food committee was appointed by the Red Cross and portable kitchens were established.

A mother and her two sons stand in what is left of their home after the May 1, 1933 tornado.

These kitchens fed approximately 500 people a day for several weeks after the storm. Due to the storm and a general shortage of funds, the school year was ended without further classes. Graduation exercises were cancelled and diplomas were given to the seniors of 1933 in the principal's office. At the same time, the next school year, 1933–34, was also shortened to seven months, and its opening was delayed until October to allow for recovery to get underway.

I will close this article in the same way I closed my article on this topic in the *North Louisiana Historical Association Journal* twenty-five years ago:

> *The tragedies of 1933 are forgotten or unknown to all but the older citizens of Minden. But those who were in Minden in 1933 remember. Is it possible the Confederate soldier of stone, still standing in the park, remembers, too? How could anyone living in Minden forget the year 1933? It was the year the "north part burned, the middle went broke, and the south part blew away," but the town still lived.*

CHAPTER 11
THE 1933 SHERIFF'S ELECTION

In the previous "Echo of Our Past," I discussed the traumatic year of 1933 in Minden. This column will focus on a brief aspect of that year: the intense race for the office of sheriff that took place in May and June of that year. From beginning to end, the race lasted approximately four weeks. Today, that is not enough time for the campaign literature to be printed. Yet the credentials of the candidates and even the statewide implications of that race have probably never been exceeded in a race for the top law enforcement officer in Minden.

Sheriff A.M. Hough was elected to office in 1928. After finishing a successful first term, he was reelected in 1932. Unfortunately, a few weeks after taking office, he came down with a case of influenza that led to further complications and produced a life-threatening illness. Hough's illness extended to several months in length, and in his absence, leadership at the Webster Parish Sheriff's Office was shared between Chief Criminal Deputy O.H. Haynes Sr.; Civil Deputy Jimmy Davis, who filled in as chief administrator; and the sheriff's son, Deputy P.M. Hough, who supervised the parish prisoners. When the devastating tornado struck Minden on Monday, May 1, 1933, Sheriff A.M. Hough's condition had deteriorated to such a degree that his doctors gave him a few days to live. True to their diagnosis, A.M. Hough died on Sunday, May 7, 1933, at the age of fifty-nine. Under state law, parish coroner Dr. S.M. Richardson assumed the office of sheriff, but the day-to-day operation of the office remained under control of the unofficial arrangement used over the months of Hough's illness. The governor had up to sixty days to call a special election and then the date for the Democratic primary, to precede the general election, would be set by the Parish Democratic Executive Committee. (The Republican Parish Committee would have also set a date for a Republican primary if a Republican Party had existed in Webster Parish in 1933.)

By Friday, May 12, Governor O.K. Allen had issued the call for the special election to be held on Tuesday, June 20, 1933. The speed with which the governor issued the call raised eyebrows locally, as it normally took several weeks to get a proclamation from Baton Rouge. Speculation began that perhaps the state administration, part of the Long political organization, had a special interest in the local race. Once the date for the general election was set, the Parish Democratic Executive Committee scheduled the Democratic primary election for Tuesday, June 6, 1933. With the election dates so near, filing for the office of sheriff would open on Monday, May 15, and close on May 19. Several candidates were expected to enter the contest.

Speculation about the Long machine's interest in the local sheriff's race was heightened when the first candidate filed for the office of sheriff. He was Louie A. Jones, a Minden native, who was at that time serving as assistant superintendent of the State Highway Patrol. Jones had been with the Highway Patrol for five years, but had spent most of that time attached as the top personal bodyguard for Governor Huey P. Long. Local tradition is that Jones earned his place with Long in 1928, when as a new member of the Highway Patrol, he removed a heckler from a speech Long was delivering here in Minden during his campaign for governor. Impressed by the young lawman's actions, Long had Jones assigned to his personal staff soon after winning the office of governor. Jones rose to become one of Long's closest aides.

When Long moved on to the Senate in late 1932, Jones was promoted to assistant superintendent of the Highway Patrol, but maintained his offices here in Minden in the People's Bank building. The rapid entry of Jones into the race sparked speculation that the Long team hoped a Jones victory might finally deliver Webster Parish into the Long camp. In those years, the sheriff was the undisputed political leader of the parish, and Webster Parish, while having strong Long supporters in the rural areas, had remained, particularly in Minden, anti-Long territory. In his announcement, Jones hoped to squelch those rumors with the following comments: "The decision to enter the campaign is at the solicitation of hundreds of friends and supporters in Webster Parish where he was born and reared. Mr. Jones states that no political alliance with anyone has been made nor will any be entered into and that if elected he will be free to employ the most efficient help that can be had, without the influence of political pressure." Jones, who made the most use of paid newspaper advertising in the campaign, used as his slogan: "Efficiency and Economy." He promised to operate the sheriff's office with as few assistants as possible and with "consideration to the taxpayers at the forefront at all times."

The second candidate to file for the Democratic primary was somewhat of a surprise entry. J.D. Huckaby, president of the Webster Parish Police Jury, announced that he was running to fill the unexpired term of Sheriff Hough. Huckaby said that he too had been urged by many friends to enter the race, based upon his knowledge of the needs of the parish from his time serving on the police jury. Elected to the jury from Ward 4 in a special election in January 1929, Huckaby had filled the seat of jury president J.H. Nelson, who had resigned because of business commitments. Huckaby had then been chosen jury president himself in March 1931. In his announcement, Huckaby stressed his intimate knowledge of the financial straits of the parish, and his ability to deal with these problems while still providing the protection of the sheriff's office. Avoiding any mention of his lack of experience in law enforcement, the candidate also emphasized that he was an independent candidate with no ties to any faction. He promised to "treat everyone fairly and courteously in the enforcement of my official duties. I intend to show favoritism to none and to enforce all the laws on the statute books of Louisiana to the best of my ability and understanding, without fear, or hope of reward from any person or faction."

The third candidate to enter the race had been expected to be the leading candidate to replace Sheriff Hough. O.H. Haynes Sr. had been a deputy in the Webster Parish Sheriff's Office for several years and had served the role of chief criminal deputy since June 1932. Haynes promised continuity in the service that had been provided by the Hough administration. He planned to retain Deputy Prentiss M. Hough and promote the son of the late sheriff to chief criminal deputy. In addition, Deputy James N. Davis would retain his post as chief office deputy. In his announcement, Haynes stressed the need for efficient, economical administration of the sheriff's office and emphasized that he would enforce the laws and the economy would be practiced, not just preached.

The final entrant into the race for sheriff filed on Friday, May 19. J. Bryan Batton touted his years of experience in law enforcement and also provided a more detailed plan of action than the other candidates for the

Sheriff O.H. Haynes Sr. (front row, right) with his deputies in 1946.

position. Batton had served as chief deputy for eight years under former Sheriff "Hutch" Phillips and had also served two terms as chief of police for the City of Minden. Beginning his announcement, Batton made the seemingly obligatory disclaimer of any alliance with an outside faction and proclaimed his independence as a candidate. He, like Haynes, promised to use only one field deputy and one office deputy. Batton's other enumerated promises included charging only for the actual cost of conveying prisoners to the state penitentiary. He promised that an itemized bill would be given to the police jury and this process would save the taxpayers of the parish several thousand dollars each year. In this short campaign, this would be the nearest thing to a political attack in print issued by any candidate. Although he didn't directly levy the charge, the implication was that the current administration was costing the taxpayers those thousands of dollars that Batton would save. Since Haynes was running largely on the record of the Hough administration, Batton's statement was an indirect indictment of the Haynes campaign. Batton ended his announcement by stating that he had pleased the public in the past and, if elected, he would serve the people and enforce the law to the best of his ability.

By the time the filing ended, a little over two weeks remained before the date of the primary. After the close of filing, the Parish Democratic Executive Committee met to set the time for the election and choose the election commissioners for each voting site. The polls were to be open from 6:00 a.m. to 7:00 p.m. on Primary Day, June 6, 1933.

After the initial newspaper announcements, few ads appeared in local newspapers, and no public events were planned featuring the candidates. This race was a prime example of "retail politics," where the candidates make personal contact with as many voters as possible, a task made very difficult by the compressed time frame of this race. Newspaper articles did give clues that this was a heated race, even though no stories directly addressed what was taking place in the campaign wars. One banner headline read "Race for Sheriff Grows Tense," but the accompanying article only rehashed the biographies and promises of the four candidates. Another clue that voter interest was high came in the form of a prediction of a voter turnout approaching 2,400 of the 3,500 registered voters in Webster Parish. In those days, as today, a nearly 70 percent turnout is a sign of a hotly contested race.

On Election Day, Tuesday, June 6, even those expectations were exceeded. In the parish, 2,939 ballots were cast, or more than 80 percent of those eligible to vote. In a surprising turn of events, one candidate was able to gain a majority of the vote, avoiding the expected runoff election. O.H. Haynes Sr. won a plurality in twelve of the sixteen precincts, and compiled a total vote of 1,492, or 50.8 percent of the vote, avoiding a runoff by 22 votes. The only precincts that Haynes failed to carry were Doyline, where he was tied by J.D. Huckaby with 53 votes each; Yellow Pine and Sibley, which both were won by Louie Jones; and Dubberly, where Batton won a plurality. The final totals were: Haynes, 1,492, 50.8 percent; Jones, 654, 22.2 percent; Huckaby, 563, 19.1 percent; and Batton, 230, 7.8 percent.

The general election, scheduled for June 20, 1933, was, as always in those days of one-party Louisiana, anticlimactic. Only 491 individuals voted in the general election, and O.H. Haynes Sr. received 490 of those votes. One write-in ballot was cast for J.B. Batton. Haynes was sworn in as sheriff of Webster Parish on June 27, 1933, after his commission was received from Governor O.K. Allen. Haynes's victory began a new era of law enforcement in Webster Parish. He would serve as Webster Parish sheriff from 1933 until 1952, when he was defeated by J.D. Batton, a son of his 1933 opponent, J. Bryan Batton. In 1964, O.H. Haynes Jr., who had served as a deputy sheriff under his father, defeated J.D. Batton. O.H. Haynes Jr. would serve four terms as sheriff before retiring in 1980. Today, several descendants of O.H. Haynes Sr. are involved in law enforcement in Minden and northwest Louisiana.

Louie A. Jones remained involved in state government, including a stint as warden of the state prison at Angola. He was living in Baton Rouge at the time of his death in March 1965. J.D. Huckaby retained his seat on the police jury, serving out his term as president of the jury until 1936. Bryan Batton did not again gain election to office, but two of his sons, Sheriff J.D. Batton and longtime Minden city councilman and mayor Jack Batton, were active in political circles, and a grandson, the late Jimmy Batton, was also involved in local law enforcement.

This "Echo of Our Past" was a brief, exciting sheriff's race that perhaps attracted the most distinguished field of candidates in our parish's history and began the long association of the Haynes family with the office of sheriff in our parish. To close with a request, I mentioned briefly in this article an occasion when Huey Long appeared in Minden. I am seeking anyone who was present to hear the speech delivered by then Senator Long in Minden on Thursday evening, November 9, 1933. This speech was given particular significance in T. Harry Williams's landmark biography of Long; however, the local viewpoint of the story has never really been shared. If you

O.H. Haynes Jr. is sworn in as Webster Parish sheriff by Clerk of Court Clarence Wiley in 1964.

were present that night, over seventy years ago, I would like to record your memories. Even if you were not in attendance, but have heard stories about that night from family members, I would also be interested in learning about those accounts. Over the years, Huey Long spoke more than a dozen times in Minden, but for now I'm specifically interested in that one occasion.

CHAPTER 12

THE LOUISIANA ORDNANCE PLANT

One of the neglected "Echoes of Our Past" is the story of the Louisiana Ordnance Plant, later to be known as the Louisiana Army Ammunition Plant. We read of the many new uses being made of the facilities of the old plant; however, for more than half a century, the LOP, or LAAP, had the most significant economic impact of any entity in our local area. The history of the operation of the Shell Plant, as it was familiarly known, is a long and complex tale of various missions, operators and alternating periods of peak activity and closure, depending on our nation's defense needs. Only recently did I realize how the story of this important local industry was under-documented, despite quite a few excellent sources of information. This column will be a first step in recording the history of what was the most important local industry for the largest part of the twentieth century. It will deal with the selection and the immediate aftermath of the selection of Webster Parish as the home of the Louisiana Ordnance Plant.

By the spring of 1941, although the United States was still officially neutral in the European war, its actions revealed that it was already on a war footing. The Selective Service System had been reactivated and the draft had begun (my father was drafted into service in March 1941). Under terms of the Lend-Lease Act, our government was sending supplies of all kinds, including war material, to Great Britain. Local governments were clamoring for a "piece of the pie" as the National Defense Program began creating thousands of new jobs in new war-related industrial facilities. North Louisiana was anxious for its fair share of these jobs.

In early April 1941, word was received that large war games would be held in the Minden area in the late summer of 1941, and it was hoped that these activities would provide an economic boost for the area. Fourth District congressman Overton Brooks and Senators Allen Ellender and John Overton were being pressed to bring some of the military-related industries to northwest Louisiana. However, all the news regarding local prospects for such an enterprise had been bad. In February, word had been received by Congressman Brooks that a petition signed by local residents requesting a military camp to be placed in the Minden area had been rejected by the White House. The president's reply stated that Louisiana had already received its quota of military installations under the current defense plans. The local chapter of the American Legion filed another request for consideration as a campsite in March with Senator Allen Ellender. Ellender informed the local group that all potential campsites had been awarded and Minden was not on the list.

In his weekly newspaper column to his constituents, published in the *Minden Herald* of April 25, 1941, Brooks gave local residents a hint that good news finally might be coming. He reported, "For a number of months I have been working upon the matter of bringing to Northwest Louisiana a national defense industry. It has recently become known that the general area of Northwest Louisiana, South Arkansas, and East Texas has received the sanction of 'authorities that be' in Washington." The news was positive, but hopes seemed slim, as the Louisiana Congressional delegation, particularly Brooks, Ellender and Overton, lacked seniority when compared to the members of Congress from south Arkansas and east Texas. Anyone making odds on Webster Parish's chances to receive the proposed plant would have classed the possibility as a long shot. More than a month passed after Brooks's column with no sign of good news. Then, suddenly, the hard work by local officials and the congressman seemed to pay off, almost overnight.

The *Shreveport Times* of May 29, 1941, announced that Congressman Brooks had received notification from the quartermaster general of the army that a large shell-loading plant would be located near Shreveport. The site description was vague but indicated that the plant would be located outside Bossier City and east of the Red River. By Friday, May 30, the *Minden Herald* picked up on the story and found that as soon as President Roosevelt signed the authorization, the plant would be located in either rural Bossier or Webster Parish. Congressman Brooks estimated that the plant would employ ten to fifteen thousand workers and cost $25 to $30 million to build. The minimum area needed for such a facility would be ten to fifteen thousand acres. Brooks additionally assured area residents that ordnance plants such

The gates to the Louisiana Army Ammunition Plan in 1957, shown as a visiting dignitary from Brazil is welcomed.

as these were operated with extreme safety precautions and would not create an extraordinary risk for those living near the facility.

On Wednesday afternoon, June 4, 1941, President Roosevelt signed authorization for the construction of an ordnance plant west of Minden on Dorcheat Bayou. The plant would be erected at a cost of $30 million, cover twenty thousand acres and initially employ about six thousand workers. Word reached Minden at about 5:00 p.m. on that afternoon in a telegram from Congressman Brooks to Mayor Floyd D. Culbertson Jr., State Representative James E. Bolin, Lions Club president Harry Andress and the local newspapers. Later, a similar telegram was received from Senator Ellender. Ellender reported that the local site had been selected largely through local persistence and the good impression that the area and the site had made on Colonel F.H. Miles, head of the ammunition division of the ordnance section of the U.S. Army.

Friday's *Minden Herald* banner headline screamed "$30,000,000 Shell Plant for Minden." Throughout the town, community leaders sprang to life with new ideas and initiatives sparked by the good news. At the meeting of the

The gates to the LAAP reservation today, as it serves as Camp Minden of the Louisiana National Guard.

Minden Lions Club on Thursday, June 5, the day after the announcement, a movement was started to reorganize the dormant Minden Chamber of Commerce. It was felt that such an organization would be necessary with the expected influx of new residents and business that the Shell Plant would bring. At the same meeting, a local fund drive for USO activities was started under the direction of J.E. Harper.

During the next week, even more signs of the coming boom were apparent. The local office of the Louisiana State Employment Service was overrun by workers seeking both construction jobs and positions at the plant. In the absence of rent controls, most local landlords immediately raised their rental charges. On June 11, the War Department established an office in the Webster Parish Courthouse to make preliminary surveys of the site and appraisals of the value of the private property that would have to be obtained to build the plant. As an outgrowth of the Lions project to create a chamber of commerce, the city decided to create an Executive Committee to handle the many problems expected in handling the sudden burst in economic development and population. Mayor Culbertson reported that his office had received 142 visitors on Wednesday alone, all seeking information about the city. Local ministers expressed concerns, as four different inquiries had been made about the legality of slot machines in Minden.

The new Executive Committee was a quasigovernmental agency that filled the role of a chamber of commerce while also having some limited governmental authority to establish certain regulations that would automatically be approved by the town council or the police jury. The members of the Executive Committee were Chairman J.H. Nelson; Lions Club president Harry Andress; Representative James Bolin; the Reverend W.F. O'Kelley of the Minden Presbyterian Church; the Reverend J.J. Rasmussen of the First Methodist Church; Minden Bank president J.E. Harper; President of the School Board C.W. Thompson; President of the police jury Marshall Pearce; Mayor Floyd Culbertson; and Civitan president Dr. Thomas Richardson. A program formally announcing the committee was held at the Ferguson Memorial Tabernacle of the First Baptist Church on Friday night, June 20. Governor Sam Jones made the keynote address beginning the efforts toward preparing the area for the new growth. Other local communities were also preparing for the inevitable impact of the new industry. Doyline and Haughton both began the process of incorporation, as they were the two nearest communities to the proposed site.

While local preparations continued, the government's work on the project was also going full steam ahead. The contract to construct the plant was awarded to Silas Mason and Company of New York. Plans called for the Mason Company to subcontract the actual construction work to local contractors. After completion, Silas Mason would operate the plant while the government retained ownership. The $30 million contract was negotiated on a cost, plus fixed-fee basis, and the plant was to be completed by January 1, 1942. Engineering plans were already underway and it was expected that construction could begin as early as July 15.

Much of this planning was being done "on the fly" and local planning changed rapidly. By June 20, the originally proposed chamber of commerce was in its third form and had a new name, the Webster Council. Former Webster Parish superintendent of schools and president of Louisiana Tech E.S. Richardson was named executive secretary of the Webster Council. He would be in day-to-day charge of the program. His stenographer, or secretary, was Miss Zenobia Camp, later to become Mrs. Zenobia West. The Board of Directors of the council included Andress, Dr. Thomas Richardson, Pearce, Culbertson, Thompson, Nelson, Harper and Rasmussen from the previous boards. New members were Dan W. Stewart, Dr. Edmond Klamke,

Jasper Goodwill, Ed Brown, E. Henry Lowe, E.K. Berry and H.O. West. The council was to be funded by contributions from the public and from the local governmental bodies.

Preparations for the actual construction of the plant were also going forward. The manager of the Shreveport Social Security office spoke in Minden to remind workers that they must obtain a Social Security number before they would be eligible to be hired to work on the plant project. In a special meeting of the city council, the city of Minden tackled several problems. It issued a permit for a bus line to operate within the city and transport workers to the plant site and also passed Minden's first ordinance to regulate the establishment of "trailer camps" within the city. A new subdivision was announced for Homer Road, just adjacent to the existing city limits, and that land was annexed by the city. Mayor Culbertson was authorized to inquire about the possibility of getting federal help to improve the sewage system in Minden to help handle the new residents. The Webster Parish Police Jury soon followed suit in passing an ordinance regulating the trailer camps.

The Louisiana State Police announced the establishment of an office at the plant site to help with potential crime problems and to enforce the newly established speed limits of fifty-five miles per hour for autos and forty miles per hour for trucks on U.S. Highway 80 between Minden and Shreveport. A controversy had arisen over the fate of the state road that connected Doyline to U.S. Highway 80, which ran through the plant site. The chairman of the Louisiana Highway Commission assured local residents that the highway would not be closed until an alternate route could be constructed.

In late June, the Webster Council sent a delegation of E.S. Richardson, Harry Andress, J.E. Harper, Floyd Culbertson, J.E. Pitcher and Dr. Edmond Klamke to Milan, Tennessee. Milan was home to a similar ordnance plant that was nearly completed. Since Milan was a smaller community than Minden, the leaders hoped to learn how it was coping with the influx of new residents and the problems of supplying the necessary services to make the opening of the new plant run smoothly.

For the first month after the announcement of the plant, things had been going very well and no roadblocks had entered into the path of progress. However, by July 1, several problems had emerged. These problems would continue throughout the construction process and beyond. On July 1, 1941, a condemnation order was issued by the Justice Department in order to obtain the land needed for the plant site. More than three hundred families, along with three schools, several churches and six cemeteries, were in the

The administration building of the LAAP shown as it looks today.

condemned area of 15,500 acres. While most of the landowners were willing to accept the price offered by the government for their property, several large landowners would eventually file a suit charging the government with undervaluation of the property. That suit would be proceeding forward even as work on the plant began.

Another problem arose over the labor supply for the construction of the plant. J.E. Harper reported to the Lions Club that all the laborers at the plant in Milan, Tennessee, were members of unions. Here in northwest Louisiana, few workers other than the railroad employees were unionized. The local business community was strongly opposed to the introduction of unionized labor to the area. The problems over open shop versus union shop would recur during the construction. Another problem came when the War Department announced that the road connecting Doyline to Highway 80 would be closed immediately, despite promises to the contrary from the State Highway Department. Doyline residents were not pleased by this decision and complained to Baton Rouge and Washington seeking relief.

The events described in this column are a summary of what happened in just the first month after the announcement of the proposed Louisiana Ordnance Plant. As you can imagine, it will take many more "Echoes of the Past" to begin to tell the whole story of the plant. That story will involve a Congressional investigation, explosions, prosperity and economic downturns in times of military cutbacks, and will see the plant touch the majority of families in the Minden area, as few families will not have some relative work at "the plant." Future "Echoes of the Past" will continue the saga of the Louisiana Ordnance Plant, the most important industrial development in the history of Minden.

CHAPTER 13

1966: A WATERSHED YEAR

The *Press-Herald* transitioned to a daily paper on July 18, 1966. The fact that the *Press-Herald* made its change in 1966 is just another of a series of events that made 1966 a watershed year in several areas of local history. In this article, I'm going to examine a few of those events, largely dealing with the rolling back of racial barriers. If you had to list one year when the nearly century-long era of Jim Crow society came to an end in Minden, 1966 would be that year. It was the year that the world of "separate but equal" arising out of the *Plessy v. Ferguson* decision of 1896 disappeared and the southern apartheid of our nation began to fade from the local scene. It was not an overnight event, but there can be little doubt that 1966 is the year when the true change began, so it is appropriate that we look back at those aspects of 1966.

The first massive changes to Minden in 1966 came in the form of a federal court order handed down by Judge Ben C. Dawkins of the Western District of Louisiana. In November 1965, several parents of local black children had filed a suit, *Blaine A. Gilbert et al v. Webster Parish School Board*, challenging the segregated status of local schools. This suit was one of a series of suits being filed in neighboring parishes and all across the South, where the structure of the schools was almost universal in its segregated nature. As such, decisions by federal judges based in *Brown* and the Civil Rights Act of 1964 were swift and simple—the era of segregated schools must end under federal mandate. Dawkins set up guidelines in his decision announced in December 1965 and ordered that the changes begin in the spring semester, starting in January 1966.

On January 10, 1966 the Webster Parish School Board met to consider applications submitted during the previous week, January 3 through January

7, 1966, for transfer to majority white schools by black students. Under the plan approved by Judge Dawkins, the integration was to be phased in over a three-year period, with four of the twelve grades in local schools integrated each year. For the spring semester of 1966, grades one, two, eleven and twelve at the local white schools—Stewart and Richardson Elementary and Minden High School—were to be integrated. In the fall of 1966, grades three and four at Richardson and Stewart and grades nine and ten at Minden High were to integrate, with grades five and six at Richardson and Stewart and grades six, seven and eight at Lowe Junior High to follow in the fall of 1967. Although Dawkins's ruling applied to the entire parish, the plaintiffs for the suit all resided in Minden and the only changes ordered at that time were in the Minden schools.

The nature of the process was strenuous for the parents and children wanting to make the change. Applications had to be submitted and evaluated by the school board. Few tried to make the change, and when integration did take place it was a very small trickle, leading to the flood of change that would eventually follow in the next decade.

Integration first came to the schools of Minden on the morning of Monday, January 17, 1966. Here is the special account from the *Minden Press* of that afternoon:

> *Color bars in three local schools were lowered quietly without incident today as five Negro students entered Minden High, Stewart Elementary and Richardson Elementary Schools for the first time.*
>
> *All five students arrived at the school shortly after 8 a.m. today in the company of their parents. Principals talked to the enrollees and their parents prior to placing the students in assigned classes.*
>
> *Two are enrolled at Minden High and Stewart and one transferred to Richardson. A sixth student, Shirley D. Lewis was approved for transfer but did not report to Stewart this morning.*
>
> *Others making the transfer included: Beverly L. Hampton, second grade from J.L. Jones to Richardson; Blaine A. Gilbert, first grade from Jerry A. Moore School to Stewart; Roslyn A. Hill, second grade, from Moore to Stewart; Elroy Allums, senior, from Webster High to Minden High; and George Washington, Jr., junior, from Webster High to Minden High.*
>
> *The five transferred under terms of a court order requiring the school board to desegregate grades one, two, 11 and 12 this term. The order calls for grades three, four, nine and 10 next fall and the final four grades in the fall of 1967.*

No other schools in the parish currently are involved in any transfers. However the court order involves the entire parish school system.

I was a student in one of the first integrated classrooms, that of Miss Audrey Hortman at Richardson Elementary. Beverly Hampton was my new classmate and later that year, as you will read, her father, J.D. Hampton, would break new ground in local politics as a candidate for mayor in the Democratic primary. Another student in that room was Lee Colten, son of the former publisher of the *Minden Press* and *Minden Herald*, Tom Colten, a man whose election that fall as Minden's new mayor as a Republican would be another first for Minden.

Beverly's transfer had been the only one strongly questioned by the school board, because of the distance from her home to Richardson, which was much farther than her former school at Jones. (I might add that I was attending Richardson also as a matter of parental choice and I lived farther away from Richardson than did Beverly.) Eventually, the move was approved and she joined the other new students in our school. I cannot imagine the pressure she must have felt as the only black child in an all-white school, but

Tom Colten, elected Republican mayor of Minden in 1966, symbolically riding the Democrat donkey to celebrate his victory.

she survived. Ten years later, in 1976, she and Roslyn Hill, who was one of two to break the color barrier at Stewart that same day, were among my fellow graduates at Minden High School. We had all come through the final completion of integration of local schools—the partial integrations of 1966 and 1967, a larger integration in 1969, expanded faculty integration in 1971 and finally complete integration in the summer of 1974, when we at MHS received the entire student body of Webster High School as new classmates. Again, it all began in that watershed year of 1966, when school segregation began to crumble in Minden.

The next change, although largely symbolic, came when one of the most controversial figures of the local civil rights era, Parish Registrar of Voters Winnice P. Clement, retired in April. Here is her story excerpted from her retirement article in the *Minden Herald* of April 28, 1966:

> *Mrs. Winnice Clement's announced plans to resign from her post as Webster Parish Registrar of Voters after almost 26 years of service probably brought a variety of reactions, both here and as far away as Washington, D.C.*
>
> *To some, her May 1 resignation date is as welcome as the announcement of World War III; but to others—especially Federal agents scattered from here to the nation's capital—it probably will be more like the end of World War II after crossing verbal swords with her and her attorneys for the past nine years.*
>
> *Though the registrar's office has probably been known principally as a battle ground in the past decade, she recalls it was not always that way. She said the job did not become difficult until 1956, when an all-out effort was started to hike Negro voter registration.* [At this point I feel compelled to point out that the actual effort that began in 1956 was by the White Citizens' Council to remove black voters from the rolls. It was that controversy that prompted Governor Robert Kennon to fire Mrs. Clement in May 1956 and Governor Earl Long to reinstate her. The effort to increase black registration began in earnest in 1958.] *Since that time the office has been the battle ground with Mrs. Clement caught between the pressures of staunch segregationists on one side and the power of the Federal government on the other.*
>
> *When she took office in 1940, there were 7,002 persons registered to vote, none of whom were Negro. By October 1956, the registration had climbed to 12,957 whites and 1,775 Negroes. However, the regular four-year purge of voter rolls required under periodic registration came about*

> *two months later, setting the stage for a civil rights court battle that was not concluded until the Fall of 1963.*
>
> *The lengthy court battle, which included investigations and counter-investigations and suits and counter-suits, finally ground to a halt in the Fall of 1963 when Judge Ben C. Dawkins, Jr., enjoined Mrs. Clement from any discriminatory practices in processing voter applications, including the use of any examination.*

Although Mrs. Clement's departure was largely symbolic and the implementation of the Voting Rights Act of 1965 the previous August had opened the registration process to all on an equal basis, the absence of such a visible figure from the voter registration battle in Webster Parish was another sign of the changes to come. At the peak of the crisis, black voting registration in Webster Parish had dropped to around 120 people in 1962. As we will see, that number mushroomed after the Voting Rights Act took effect.

That change in voting rolls was demonstrated by the next watershed moment, the municipal Democratic primary in August 1965. For those of you who have come to Louisiana after 1975 and the birth of Edwin Edwards's "Cajun Primary," yes, Louisiana once had a "normal" election process that included party primary elections. This marked the first local election since the numbers of black voters had increased, and a concerted effort to encourage black voter participation had taken place in Minden.

One of the first changes came in those election officials who oversee the balloting in each precinct, the commissioners. Even during the years of Reconstruction, when black elected officials served for about fifteen years in the Minden town government and briefly in the parish government, the mechanism of the election had always been completely white. No blacks had been allowed to exercise any authority in the supervision of the elections and certainly not in the counting of ballots. Anyone familiar with the legacy of the Returning Board and the dual sets of election returns in Louisiana's Reconstruction history understands why that was not allowed in a parish such as Webster, which was under Redeemer Democrat control.

With that background, the first edition of a daily *Minden Press-Herald*, issued on Monday, July 18, 1966, had a headline that I'm sure many white Mindenites never expected to read: "Six Negroes Drawn for Commissioner Service." At that time in Webster Parish, commissioners' names were drawn by lot from those submitted by candidates. Each candidate was allowed to submit a list for each precinct in which they were scheduled to campaign.

Webster Parish Democratic Executive Committee chairman Henry Hobbs reported that "eight Negroes were drawn during Saturday's commissioner selection session. However, two of the eight were declared ineligible because they live outside Minden."

The candidate who submitted the prospective black commissioners was a man who had already shocked many local voters when he had earlier filed to be a candidate. Challenging two-term incumbent mayor Frank Norman was J.D. Hampton, father of my classmate Beverly Hampton and one of the plaintiffs on the desegregation suit that had changed local schools. Hampton's official campaign announcement, which appeared in the *Minden Press-Herald* on July 20, 1966, was as follows:

> *J.D. Hampton, Jr.*
>
> *I was born in Webster Parish 31 years ago and have been a resident of Minden for the last 15 years, along with my wife and 3 children. I am a graduate of Webster High School, a veteran, and am presently employed by the LAAP. For the past year, I have been chairman of the United Christian Freedom Movement and am a member of Mt. Zion CME church.*
>
> *I am asking for your support because I believe that we need a better mayor for a better Minden. We need a concerned mayor, a mayor who is interested in everybody's problems, an active mayor who is on the spot when anything happens and who works a full day every day. We need a mayor who has the experience and the desire to aid the people of Minden whenever they need assistance.*
>
> *Above all, we need a mayor for all the people. I do not believe either in "black power" or in "white power," but rather in the power held by all the people, which is expressed throughout their elected representatives. If elected, I would not be a "Negro mayor" for Negroes, nor would I be controlled by any special group. I would instead be a mayor of Minden for all the people of Minden.*
>
> *I believe that we can build a better Minden. We can have a Minden where problems are handled with firm leadership and understanding. This has not been the case to date. For example, last September the present mayor fired 19 of the city's garbage collectors because they requested a pay raise. Garbage collection was then allowed to deteriorate at the hands of prisoners and inexperienced employees, and the city had to hire its new employees at an increased rate of pay. This injury to the citizens of Minden, and to the city's former employees could easily have been avoided had the mayor made any attempt to negotiate a reasonable settlement. Furthermore, we all know*

that this city lacks recreational facilities for our children, who spend too much of their time roaming the streets and who all too often end up in court. The present mayor has failed to take the lead in mobilizing the city council, the recreation committee, and all interested citizens to develop programs and facilities which will keep our youth active and safe.

Most important, we can have a Minden where the mayor takes the lead in making every possible effort to attract new industry. My election alone will prove to manufacturers that Minden is indeed the "friendliest city in the South." And I promise that no opportunity will be missed to bring new jobs and new prosperity to our city.

Minden has a great future. We need a better mayor for a better Minden. Vote Hampton—Number 36 on August 13.

In the same issue, Mayor Norman issued his own official announcement:

Frank T. Norman

I have lived in Minden and Webster Parish all of my life. I received my education at Minden High School, Ringland College and Louisiana Tech.

I was married to the former Mildred Bryant of Simsboro, Louisiana on August 1, 1937. We have one daughter, Frankie, who also graduated from Minden High School and Louisiana Tech. She is now married to Ray Tompkins and they have two children, Norman, age 5 and Janet, age 3.

I am a member of the First Baptist Church and have served from time to time on the official board.

I am a member of the Lions Club.

I am presently serving on the board of directors of Minden Industrial Development Corporation.

I am a member of practically all bodies of the Masonic Lodge, both York and Scottish Rite. I am now serving as Grand Commander of the Grand Commandery of Louisiana. I am also a member of the Knights of Pythias and the Woodmen of the World.

I was elected to the City Council in 1952 and served two terms as Public Safety Commissioner. I was elected Mayor in 1958. Since that time Minden has grown tremendously—both in population and in industries. Since then I have worked very closely with the State Municipal Association and I received much knowledge beneficial to the operation of a municipality, having served as President of the Louisiana Municipal Association in 1964. By observing the progress and growth of the city, both in its operation and otherwise, I believe my record will stand on its own merits.

> *I am asking you to again elect me to the office of Mayor of Minden and I pledge my continued efforts in trying to make this the best place in the world to live. I am deeply grateful for the confidence that you have given me in the past and I humbly ask for your continued support. Vote for No. 37 on the ballot.*

The campaign was not as tempestuous as Hampton's announcement statement might have indicated. Hampered by a lack of funds, his campaign advertising largely consisted of a small ad that appeared in the local newspaper on several occasions. It featured his picture and the following text: "Vote for—More recreation—More industry—More leadership—J.D. Hampton, Jr. for Mayor, No. 36—A Better Mayor for a Better Minden."

While no one ever thought Hampton could win the primary, Norman and many in Minden seemed to pretend as if he did not even exist. The *Press-Herald*, in its election coverage, never again mentioned Hampton's name in a news story, only mentioning that the mayor's race was on the ballot. In the few ads that Norman ran in the newspaper, he didn't advance a platform or even mention having an opponent. He merely asked voters to exercise the right to vote on August 13.

There were some indications that while there was little chance that Hampton could win the election, the vote totals might surprise some casual observers. The first was a general dissatisfaction with the way things were going in local government. That would be reflected more in the general election later in the year, when Norman would be defeated. But it was also very clear that the voting population for this election would be very different from the one that had voted in 1962, at a time when just over 100 blacks were eligible to vote in all of Webster Parish. The new registrar of voters reported the following to the *Minden Press-Herald*: "Preliminary figures show that 5,411 persons are qualified to vote in the city election. This is almost double the number of voters who were eligible to vote in the 1962 city election. By the end of June…1,680 Negroes were registered to vote in the City of Minden and an additional 106 Negroes registered during July prior to the deadline, although some of these may not reside in Minden."

A record number of absentee votes for the city, more than 200, were cast in the days leading up to the election. When the votes were tallied on the night of August 13, Mayor Norman had gained reelection with 2,729 votes to Hampton's 1,164, or 70 percent to 30 percent, a landslide victory. But it was truly amazing when you consider that Hampton's vote total was about ten times the number of blacks who were even registered to vote less than a

Mayor Tom Colten and the new city council being sworn into office in 1967.

year earlier. Hampton had carried four of the ten precincts in Minden and, even more surprisingly, had gained votes in all ten, even one that had an all-white voter base. Truly this was an indication that Minden's politics had left the Jim Crow era and were moving toward the place we are today. It would be more than a decade, and yet another federal court order eliminating the commission form of government and mandating redistricting, before we would elect a black city official, and we still have not elected a black mayor. But today, black voters play an active role in our local politics, as should be expected in the United States. As of July 7, there are 4,006 registered black voters in Minden, or 46 percent of the voting population. That move toward all citizens having an equal chance to participate in Minden city government began with the events of 1966.

In the general election, Norman would lose the race to Republican Tom Colten, the first Republican elected to office in Webster Parish since Reconstruction—yet another sign of the changes in our society that were emerging in 1966.

So as you can see, while 1966 is a very significant year for the *Minden Press-Herald* as it came into existence as a daily paper, in a greater way, 1966 was the year that many of our fellow citizens became full participants in the local community for the first time.

CHAPTER 14

THE DORCHEAT HISTORICAL ASSOCIATION MUSEUM

On Tuesday, November 13, 2007, I had the privilege of attending a very special event here in Minden. Called "A Night at the Museum," it was a sneak preview of the Dorcheat Historical Association Museum for contributors. While the museum is not yet ready for a public viewing, I thought I would use this column to provide a word picture of where the progress stands, although words don't do the work that has been completed justice.

The design of the museum will take the visitor on a journey telling the story of Webster Parish from the time Europeans first came to the area, tracing the development of communities and culture and highlighting the achievements of local residents. That is a strong theme in the museum, as Executive Director Schelley Brown commented at the event: the large number of people who have achieved success at the highest levels of all areas of life from Webster Parish remind the children of today that truly they can reach any goal for which they strive.

Entering the museum is quite a surprise for those familiar with the previous efforts those of us in the Dorcheat Historical Association have made toward a museum. While our attempts were sincerely motivated and did provide a chance to highlight some of our heritage, those efforts lacked a few things that are now present. First, the organization and drive provided by having a hands-on person tasked with promoting and developing the museum, Schelley Brown. Second, the persistent leadership ability of our president, Thad Andress, which moved our fundraising to a new level. Finally, and perhaps most significant, is the artistic genius and hard work of Larry Milford. The result is something unlike what you've seen in Minden in the

Native American display case at the Dorcheat Historical Association Museum.

past, a presentation equal to the scope of our story. A museum that will make our town proud and bring people to see our history portrayed.

When completed, the cases and displays will form a path that will allow one to stroll and move forward in time from those early beginnings over two hundred years ago to the present. The mixture of tangible artifacts of the past, combined with words telling the story and moving images of art, will make visitors feel as if they have "lived" our history. At present, the first few displays are completed and I will describe them to let you see what is in store.

Entering the museum, you will be overwhelmed by the first display case, both by the content and by the sheer size and beauty of the cabinet. You will find yourself face to face with Native Americans, just as Freeman and Custis did in 1806 when they found their way into Bayou Dorcheat after being diverted by the Great River Raft in the Red. (And perhaps just as Bienville did over a century earlier in 1701—a possibility not yet proven but one that seems likely from some of his journals.) The accompanying artwork and information tells the story of the Caddo people, who were the indigenous population here at the time of European migration. As in the rest of the museum, artifacts, such as arrowheads, are mixed with realistic, accurate images of the lives of our earliest residents.

However, don't be so stunned by that case that you fail to glance to your right and see on the southern wall of the building a ceiling-to-floor map of Webster Parish, showing the earliest settlements and their dates of founding. I had the occasion to speak with several local residents at the event who were not aware of the exact locations of those settlements and the early settlement dates of some areas. Alongside the map are spectacular images of the scenic beauty of Webster Parish.

Moving forward, on the west wall of the building you encounter recreations of the earliest European settlements in the area, including a recreation of Newitt Drew's gristmill at the junction of Cooley Creek and Dorcheat Bayou. That enterprise, established in the mid-1820s, led to the emergence of Overton, the pioneer community that became the seat of government for old Claiborne Parish before succumbing, like so many of its residents, to the yellow fever and malaria that were products of its low-lying location. You will find yourself on the dock at Overton as a large steamboat comes chugging in and you will feel as if you have been transported by the combination of realistic art and sounds and actual artifacts, some of which first came to our area at Overton more than 150 years ago. Next to the dock you will see the tombstone of a pioneer settler who made the trek from Pennsylvania to Overton, where he died (allowing the tombstone to make quite a trek itself, all the way to a book room at Minden High School). The image of the steamboat, long the symbol of the Dorcheat Association, is the trademark image of our museum.

In the corner of the room, you will find a reconstruction of a cabin, typical of those constructed by both the hardy Scots-Irish settlers who came west after the Indian Removal Acts of the 1830s and the German Utopians who settled at Germantown. The cabin is constructed from the actual timbers of the O'Bier Home, a historic dwelling of the 1850s that was moved from its original Shongaloo location to Germantown in the 1970s. Unfortunately, termite infestation required the home to be taken down a few years ago, but the salvageable lumber was saved and now that memory is preserved and gives museum visitors a wonderful taste of authenticity. Entering the cabin will take you back to life in those early years as you look at the sparse furnishings of frontier life.

Moving to the east, you will come to the beginnings of the story of schools in Webster Parish. This is a work in progress, but it already contains memorabilia from famous athletes who honed their craft in Webster Parish schools, such as Louis Dunbar and John David Crow, and images and

Caddo Indian display and mural at the Dorcheat Historical Association Museum.

Recreation of the dock at Overton in the Dorcheat Historical Association Museum.

The Dorcheat Historical Association Museum's reconstructed 1840s-style cabin is built from lumber taken from the 1850 O'Bier House, formerly stored at the Germantown Colony Museum.

artifacts from classrooms and the music programs of the schools. Much more will come later.

To the north is a section portraying the impact of religion in our area, highlighting the work of the prominent Baptist hymn writer B.B. McKinney of South Webster Parish and including an old church pew (prior to the time when cushions were added for comfort and, I guess, better sleeping for some of us who are inattentive).

Perhaps the most discussed part of the exhibit is to the west on the back side of the Indian display case, where achievements of famous folks with Webster Parish ties are displayed. Items have been sent from people such as Alan Bean, the astronaut and "moon walker" whose brief time as a Minden resident was preserved by his image as mascot of the Minden High School band. Other items have been donated by musicians such as James Burton and Trace Adkins, while memorabilia of older local entertainers like Percy Mayfield and Gene Austin are on display.

Moving around to the south side of the Indian case, there is a small display about a topic largely unknown to many who reside here: the story of the saltworks in South Webster Parish, a natural resource that helped bring Native Americans to the area and was a focus of enterprise, particularly during the Civil War years.

That finishes my brief tour, but let me emphasize that by no means have I described everything already in place. In fact, I'm not sure I saw everything that is already on display. All around on the walls are images from our past, historic maps and various pieces of nostalgia that I saw locals standing around and discussing. Also, if this doesn't sound like "much" to some of you, I need to tell you, first, that the quality of the displays will let you see how much painstaking effort is being put into making this a first-class museum, which takes time, and second, "you ain't seen nothing yet." The only thing holding us back is time and money—but both of those obstacles will be "licked."

When completed, the Dorcheat Historical Association Museum will be the finest local museum in the state of Louisiana, and I say that without hesitation. It will be something that Minden and all of Webster Parish will truly be proud to have and will be an attraction for tourists with ties to the parish and even casual observers. It is that very reason that led the Webster Parish Convention and Visitors Bureau to make a key grant that allowed much of the present work to take place. But those are dollars that will be returned to the local economy multiple times by the museum.

My good Republican friends here often kid me about my politics, but it is now my turn to kid them. I hope they all contributed enough to our new governor that he will look favorably to future funding for the museum from the State Department of Tourism, Culture and Recreation. Those funds will allow the museum to expand even beyond the original scope we had planned years ago, to include facilities that will allow the educational role of the museum to add a dimension to the study of history and culture in local schools that we've never been able to provide.

So I hope I've inspired some of you to pitch in and help in this effort. Money is not what we are about, but money is needed to build a quality museum. While some members of the association will probably let you have a sneak peek for free, I can assure you we'd like nothing better than to give you a preview when you become a contributor to the museum and part of the association as we move forward in preserving the past. As someone who has spent so many years hoping to see this come to pass, I am excited and thrilled of the statement this museum will make about our community. Won't you join us?

AUTHOR'S NOTE: In the eighteen months since this article was published, the museum has advanced beyond our wildest dreams. The entire front room of the museum is now filled with exhibits highlighting our history, and we at the museum are about to embark on turning the back room into an educational center to promote the study of our past. It is truly an irreplaceable asset in preserving and learning from our local history.

CHAPTER 15

THE GERMANTOWN STORY

As reported in Wednesday's *Press-Herald*, the last few weeks of the summer of 2008 have been full of good news for the Germantown Colony Museum. After decades of limping along on slim financial support, the recent decision to turn the property over to the secretary of state's office, if approved by the legislature, will finally give the wonderful heritage of the colony to be displayed and applied to teach the lessons to future generations. Today, I am repeating a brief history of the Germantown colony.

During the early years of the nineteenth century, European society was in turmoil. Old national orders such as the French Empire had fallen. A charismatic leader, Napoleon, threatened to unite the entire continent under his control. Throughout the region, the accepted loyalties to local rulers and institutions were under question. Thinking men in all areas of the continent began to reexamine the entire structure of the social, political and economic order. This questioning was particularly prevalent in areas of the old Holy Roman Empire that are today part of the modern nation of Germany. The residents of the area around the province of Württemberg were mostly members of the Roman Catholic Church. The Catholic faith was predominant throughout most of what is now southern and western Germany. It was in Württemberg that the questioning of the old order led to the emergence of an organized movement within the Catholic Church to restructure society. This movement became known as the Harmonist Society.

Under the leadership of George Rapp, the Harmonists would found several settlements in the United States during the first half of the nineteenth century. These settlements intended to put into practice the utopian ideals taught by Rapp and other leaders. Three major settlements were eventually founded; scholars have researched and documented the history of the first two, New Harmony, Indiana, and Economy, Pennsylvania, and established their places in our social and economic history. Unfortunately, scholars have neglected the third settlement, the Germantown colony of Louisiana, which was ironically the longest-lived of the trio. The volumes of work done on the New Harmony and Economy settlements have largely documented the ideals of these colonists. The purpose of this article is to add illumination to the story of Germantown, its own leader, the mystic Count Leon, and help establish Germantown's rightful place as an equal partner with the two better-known German religious utopian experiments.

Monarchs of the tiny kingdoms in the German-speaking areas of Europe viewed these religious utopians as threats to their power. As the era of revolution would show, these small kingdoms were obsolete relics of feudalism and were open to such threats. However, the small-sized Utopian movement proved easier to control than the widespread democratic movements that arose later. Government officials simply asked Rapp and his followers to leave the country or give up their ideas. They came to the United States, where they first settled in Butler County, Pennsylvania, before relocating to southern Indiana, where the Harmony settlement was founded in 1814. Rapp and his followers remained at this site until 1825, when the Scottish idealist Robert Owen bought the town. The Rappites returned to Pennsylvania and established the Economy community north of Pittsburgh. Owen renamed the Indiana settlement New Harmony, removed the religious aspects of the communal living system and shifted the emphasis of the community to literary and cultural pursuits. The society went out of existence in the 1850s. Rapp's Economy colony flourished for a few years but fell to internal squabbles before the Civil War. But what of Germantown—how was it created and what makes it significant?

In 1831, a unique figure arrived in the Economy colony with his followers. This man was known by several names: Maximilian Bernhard Ludwig, Bernhard Müller, Maximilian Bernhard Lewis, Count Maximilian Leon Proli and several other titles, including the "Lion of Judah." However, his followers knew him as Count Leon, and that is the title we will use. Leon was the uncle of Empress Marie Louise of Austria, the second wife of Napoleon, and had ties to royalty throughout Europe. He used these ties to stay in Europe long after authorities had expelled most other Utopians. He eventually gained a devoted group of followers who followed him to the United States. Interestingly, Leon had just settled his disputes with local monarchs and said the leading of God caused his departure to the United

One of the restored buildings at the Germantown Colony Museum.

States. A vision he received in 1816 revealed to Leon his role as a prophet. By the time of his departure for America, Leon had about one hundred followers, including such prominent and learned men as Dr. George Goentgen, who had been chief librarian of the city of Frankfurt. What did these followers of Leon believe? Their doctrine in detail is a complex and organized system of intricate tenets given by their leader. A brief summary of Leon's ideas would include the following ideas: A new world order will replace the existing world society, signaling the beginning of the millennium era referred to in the Bible. In preparation for the coming new era, of which Count Leon is to be the leader, believers should organize themselves into communal settlements. In these colonies, believers would share all in common and await the return of the Lord and the start of the millennium. Leon said that God had revealed to him that Christ would return first to North America and establish the true Christian church there because of the freedom of religion in the United States.

Leon contacted Rapp in Pennsylvania and asked to join the colony. He expressed his views to the older leader, and Rapp was receptive because many of Leon's ideas coincided with his own. He welcomed Leon to Economy. Unfortunately, soon after Leon arrived, his charisma attracted a following among the community residents that rivaled Rapp's. As Leon's support grew, a civil war erupted in the colony. The battle spilled over into the courts and led to a separation. Leon and his followers, who now numbered almost a third of the colony, along with a court award of $105,000, left Economy and established the city of Phillipsburg on the Ohio River in 1832. This group, called the New Philadelphia Congregation, built many impressive brick buildings at the site, which is today the town of Monaca, Pennsylvania. Economic problems arose at Phillipsburg, largely caused by Leon's reliance on religious tenets and his failure to grasp financial realities. Under the threat of additional lawsuits, Leon decided to remove his followers to a new location, farther west and closer to the latitude of Jerusalem.

On September 1, 1833, Leon and his followers started down the Ohio River in search of a locality nearer to the place where God would reveal himself. On February 4, 1834, the party landed at Grand Ecore, Louisiana, on the Red River, opening the final saga of their journey. This first Louisiana site, while closer to Biblical latitudes, was unhealthy. An epidemic of yellow fever broke out and claimed many members of the settlement. Most notable of the victims was Count Leon himself, who died on August 29, 1834. His death, strangely enough, probably extended the life of the colony. The remaining settlers attempted to stay at the Grand Ecore site, which they renamed as Gethsemane. However, the unhealthy conditions, combined with flooding that destroyed much of the settlements, including the cemetery, forced them to relocate.

In 1835, the colonists bought land farther north in Claiborne Parish on high ground removed from the river. This was hilly land much like their home territory in Germany. The site, a few miles north of the present-day city of Minden, was the final home of the colony. The city of Minden was founded later, in 1836 or 1837, by Charles Veeder of New York, who had a German family background. Some historical evidence indicates that Veeder met the Germantown settlers in Kentucky as they headed down the Ohio River. This contact might have influenced his choice of a site for a town, since he came to the area with a steamboat load of goods for sale, suggesting that he had some knowledge that settlers were already in the area.

At Germantown, freed from the control of the overly idealistic Leon, the colony began to prosper. Leon's widow, the Countess Leon, Dr. Goentgen and John Bopp, the business manager, assumed the leadership of the colony. While the colonists were still bound by their earlier pledges to follow the religious teachings of Count Leon, the day-to-day operation of the settlement took on a more practical edge and became very successful. Cotton was planted and the leadership carried on fairly extensive real estate deals. A community store became the center of the life of the colony, and the communal experiment continued. The town featured five houses besides the bachelors' quarters for the unmarried men. (An interesting religious teaching of Leon forbade marriage until the return of Christ; this teaching was later ignored by the colony.) Other buildings included the store, a community kitchen, a school taught first by Goentgen and later by William Stakowsky and several barns, work sheds and outbuildings. The colony had its own shoemaker, tinsmith, smokehouse, cotton gin, sawmill, carpentry shop, blacksmith and even its own saloon. Settlers planted fruit orchards and grew mulberry trees. The mulberry leaves were used to feed silkworms that produced thread used to make cloth. The community raised sheep, cattle, chickens, geese and other animals. The colony was a self-sufficient island. In fact, the products of the colony were exported to the nearby community of Minden, including peach brandy made from the fruit in the colony's orchards.

Perhaps the most significant export of the colony to its frontier neighbors was culture. The members of the community were educated and trained in all areas of the arts. Dr. Goentgen had an impressive library that unfortunately was lost after the colony went out of business. The countess was a trained musician who wrote beautifully handwritten musical scores to avoid the cost of commercially printed music. She designed a practice board called a digitorium that she used to teach piano to her students before the colony could get a real instrument. After a piano was obtained, she taught many young ladies of Minden how to play. Later, Mr. Stakowsky began traveling to Minden on a regular schedule to teach music lessons to the residents of Germantown's neighboring community. These Europeans brought a little of the culture of the Old World to this frontier outpost. The members of the colony continued to practice communal living. Each member had his or her role in the community and each shared in the fruits of the colony's efforts. Community wells and washhouses were built. The colony continued to prosper into the 1850s. During these years, a new settler, Dr. F.O. Krouse, came to the colony and shared the business management of the colony with Bopp. The economic stability of the colony for all these years is one of its outstanding qualities.

In 1861, the Civil War broke out, and this conflict that split our nation also proved to be the death of the Germantown colony. Germantown settlers never owned slaves but took no official side during the war. While the colony welcomed and sheltered deserters and fugitives from the Confederate army, some of its most prominent members, including Dr. Krouse, joined

The ruins of the old kitchen at the Germantown colony in 1940, before the restoration of the colony.

the Southern forces. The differences that began at this time only widened as war continued. After the war ended, the economy of the South was ruined. The hard economic times spelled an end for the experiment in communal living. In 1871, a financial settlement was made between the members, and the Germantown colony formally disbanded. Most members remained in the area and set up individual homesteads. The land where the colony sat became the home of the Krouse family. Descendants of this family and others still populate the area today.

After the colony disbanded, many artifacts of the original settlement were unfortunately scattered among the descendants or allowed to suffer the eroding effects of nature. In the struggle to survive the hardships of everyday life, the unique heritage of these settlers was largely forgotten. Buildings of the colony fell into disrepair. The library of Dr. Goentgen and the valuable furnishings and artwork he and the countess owned disappeared or were destroyed. It seemed that all memory of the colony might fade away. Fortunately, during the 1940s, the colony came to the attention of two individuals who can be regarded as saviors of its heritage. Dr. Karl Arndt, a professor of German language at Louisiana State University, began doing work at the colony site in the late 1930s. Although he later shifted his work to the entire Harmonist movement and Rapp in particular, he established the role of Germantown as a historical equal to the settlements at Harmony and Economy. Later, in the 1940s, Mrs. Rita Moore Krouse married a descendant of Dr. Krouse. She spent years of painstaking research finding out about both the theory and the fact behind the Germantown colony. It was largely through her efforts that the Krouse family took the lead in establishing the Germantown Colony Museum on the site of the original settlement in 1975. This historical site, under the control of the Webster Parish Police Jury, features some surviving buildings of the colony and reconstructions of other buildings.

But what is the unique nature of Germantown? Many arguments can be advanced to answer this question. Some might cite the influence on the population of Webster and Claiborne Parishes. The descendants of these cultured and hardworking people today occupy many posts of influence, particularly in the educational system. Others might cite the German heritage of the colony. In the Anglo-Saxon culture of north Louisiana, these German settlers added to the cultural mix and attracted other Germans to the area. Their lasting legacy can be seen in the human landscape and the day-to-day lifestyle of area residents today in areas such as cooking and other traditions. While these factors are important, they are not the great historical significance of Germantown.

The greatest historical significance of Germantown is its creation and existence as a religious utopian experiment. The third member of the trio of German utopian colonies, it was longer-lived and more economically successful than either of its rivals. Harmony, founded about 1814, passed to other hands by 1825 and lost its religious nature less than twenty years after its founding. Economy kept its religious nature until the early 1850s, but its entire existence was less than thirty years. Germantown managed to survive from its founding in 1836 until 1871, a lifespan of more than thirty-five years. Even in its death, it could cease operation on its own terms, not forced out of existence by creditors or outsiders. The significance of Germantown is the lesson it teaches regarding the struggles between utopian communal ideals and the economic realities of our society. The compromises that the leaders of the colony after Leon made to keep the colony prosperous make the pragmatic form of Utopia more interesting and worthwhile of study than either of its better-known sister communities.

This new opportunity to preserve the story of the colony for future generations is so very exciting to those who have worked for so many years to save the remaining buildings. It appears that this unique experiment will now not be forgotten and the scholars of the future will explore its lessons. Locally, we have done our part; now we can hope that the Louisiana legislature goes along and will assist in doing everything possible to keep the memory of Germantown alive.